WESTWARD OF FORT CUMBERLAND

Military Lots Set Off for Maryland's Revolutionary Soldiers

With

An Appended List of Revolutionary Soldiers Granted Pensions by the State of Maryland

Mary K. Meyer
Editor

HERITAGE BOOKS
2008

HERITAGE BOOKS
AN IMPRINT OF HERITAGE BOOKS, INC.

Books, CDs, and more—Worldwide

For our listing of thousands of titles see our website at
www.HeritageBooks.com

Published 2008 by
HERITAGE BOOKS, INC.
Publishing Division
100 Railroad Ave. #104
Westminster, Maryland 21157

Copyright © 1994 Mary K. Meyer

All rights reserved. No part of this book may be reproduced or transmitted in any form or by any means, electronic or mechanical, including photocopying, recording or by any information storage and retrieval system without written permission from the author, except for the inclusion of brief quotations in a review.

International Standard Book Numbers
Paperbound: 978-1-58549-528-3
Clothbound: 978-0-7884-7304-3

TABLE OF CONTENTS

Preface v

Introduction vii

Abbreviations xiii

Military Lots Drawn by Officers 1

Military Lots Drawn by Enlisted Men 7

Patented Military Lots 59

Revolutionary Soldiers granted Maryland State Pensions 91

Maryland Pension List, 1822 151

Index 169

PREFACE

The following records have been transcribed from an 1871 publication by John M. Brewer and Lewis Mayer, who, one assumes, transcribed it from original records. Unfortunately Messrs. Brewer and Mayer did not state just what set of records they used or where those records were deposited. One could surmise, however, that at that time, the original records were stored under the jusrisdiction of the Maryland Land Office.

Many changes have taken place since that time; some of the records from that office disappeared; others were removed from that depository and ended up in private collections, etc., etc. Fortunately, since the creation of the Hall of Records/Maryland State Archives and the dissolution of the Maryland Land Office per se at which time all records of the latter were transferred to the former depository, a number of records have been located, retrieved, and or accounted for.

It is obvious, on a close reading of the following records, that the transcribers had a difficult time deciphering the original handwriting. It must also be realized that in creating the original published list, the compilers employed a multi-step labor (lacking copying machine, typewriter, computer, or Lino-type) to produce the original published lists.

The reader should be very much aware that many of the names in the following list may be spelled incorrectly or the spelling wrongly interpreted. They may even have been spelled incorrectly in the original record. Therefore, one must search for every/any possible spelling or mispelling of the name for which one is searching.

Mary K. Meyer, FNGS
Editor

MILITARY LOTS WESTWARD OF FORT CUMBERLAND

INTRODUCTION

Allegany county[1] [Maryland] comprises within its limits the military lots which were awarded to the officers and soldiers of the Maryland Line for their services during the Revolution.

There are four thousand one hundred and sixty-five lots, of fifty acres each, which were laid off by Francis Deakins, appointed under a resolution passed by the General Assembly in 1787.

The survey was made under the resolution and Mr. Deakins was appointed to make the survey; he made and returned a general plot of the county westward of Fort Cumberland, on which four thousand one hundred and sixty-five lots, of fifty acres each, were laid off, besides sundry tracts which had been patented, with a distinction on the plot of lands which had been settled and improved from those that remained uncultivated, and had also returned, in two books, certificates of all the lots before mentioned[2].

The Legislature, being now possessed of the necessary information, passed an Act, November 1778: Chapter 44, "to dispose of the reserved lands westward of Fort Cumberland, and to fulfill the engagement made by this State to the officers and soldiers of the Maryland Line in the service of the United States," in which, after reciting the acts by which bounties of land had been promised for military service, an appropriation in 1781, the appointment of Mr. Deakins, and all the facts above stated: and adding that it appeared there were three hundred and 23 families settled on six hundred and thirty-six lots of the aforesaid lots, which these people had improved and cultivated, they ordained as follows, viz: That whereas, according to the most accurate account that could then be rendered by the Auditor-General, it had appeared that there had been about the number of two thousand four hundred and seventy-five soldiers entitled under the several Acts of the Legislature to the bounty of lands, and that there ought to be about one hundred lots set apart to fulfil the engagements of land to recruiting officers; the quantity of two thousand five hundred and seventy-five of the aforesaid lots should be distributed by lot among the said soldiers and their legal representatives, by a commissioner or commissioners, not exceeding three, to be appointed by the Governor and Council for that and other purposes, presently to be noticed.

This provision went to the fulfillment of all the engagements acknowledged and recited by the Act, but the Legislature thought proper to go further and proceeded to direct that part of the remaining lots should be distributed by lottery among the officers and representatives of the officers of the Maryland Line who served to the end of the war, who were killed or died of wounds received in battle, and those who died a natural death while in the service with the army, each officer or his representative to have four lots; that the lots so granted should be adjacent to those distributed among the soldiers, allowing each officer four lots; and the said lots should be distributed by lot among the said officers and their representatives by the aforesaid Commissioners, each ticket to contain four lots contiguous [sic] to each other, or as nearly so as might be. The Act directed further, that the Auditor-General should furnish the said commissioner with a list of officers and soldiers entitled aforesaid, that no draught should be made for any officer or soldier whose name was not on that list; that after the draught or lottery the name of each officer and soldier should be endorsed on the ticket containing the number or numbers which had been drawn by or for such officer or soldier, who should thereupon have an estate, in fee-simple, in the lot or lots so drawn and endorsed, without any patent, deed or grant, to be issued for that purpose. The Act also directs that a preference should be given to those settlers to purchase the six hundred and thirty-six lots by them respectively settled, to be discharged in three equal annual payments, in the years 1798, 1790, and 1791; in default of any payment the land should be liable to proclamation by any citizen of Maryland.

The Act of 1781, opening the Land office, provides for fulfilling the engagements or the intention of the State of Maryland towards its officers and soldiers. The first enacting session of that law in substance, appropriated all the lands westward of Fort Cumberland, reserved or otherwise, except so far as they were fairly covered by warrants and locations in right of American citizens and actually paid for, to the purpose of discharging the aforesaid engagements.

Under this general appropriations the lands remained until the session of April, 1787, when a resolution was passed authorizing the Governor and Council to appoint and employ some skilful person to lay out the manors and such parts of the reserves and vacant land belonging to the State, lying westward of Fort Cumberland, as he might think fit and capable of being improved, in lots of fifty Acres each.

In virtue of this resolution, Mr. Francis Deakins was appointed for the purpose therein mentioned, who, before the fall session of 1788, had finished the survey, and had returned a general plat of the county westward of Fort Cumberland.

The Legislature then passed the Act (November, 1788, c. 44) entitled "An Act to dispose of the reserved lands westward of Fort Cumberland," the different provisions of which Act have been already given.

These are the principal and most important laws which created and defined the military lots west of Cumberland.

The extreme western section of Allegany county, known

as the Two Glades Districts, is composed mostly of military lots. The town of Oakland, fifty-six miles west of Cumberland, is located on a fifty acre lot. That portion of Allegany county laid off in lots and assigned to the officers and soldiers of the Revolution, has within the last twenty years [that is since 1851] been developed by the construction of the Baltimore & Ohio Rail Road.

That section of our State, a quarter of a century since [i.e., 1846] was terra incognita, and would still have remained unknown except for that magnificent enterprise.

As the land has increased in value, the demand has become greater; titles are subjected to the legal ordeal, and the representatives of officers and soldiers are beginning to look after titles to land which they formerly thought valueless and of little importance.

Escheat patents have been obtained on many of the lots, which have been, and will continue to be, a fruitful source of litigation as the lots increase in value.

Most of the litigation that has occurred before the Commissioner of the Land Office for many years past has been from Allegany county and especially from that section in which the military lots lie. The Land Office, important to every part of the State, containing the patents and original tenures by which land is held, becomes, in Allegany county, where the titles to land are yet unsettled and disturbed, almost a vital necessity.

The Acts of the Legislature of Maryland with reference to the military district of the State are substantially given, not only the information of the heirs of the officers and soldiers of the Revolution, but as monuments to show that the State appreciated and cherished the memory of her sons who defended her cause and that of her sister States.

[1] These military lands were in the original county of Allegany. In 1872 Garrett county was created out of the western part of Allegany county.

[2] Francis Deakins drew several maps of the Military Lands showing the numbered lots. Copies may be obtained from the Maryland State Archives, 350 Rowe Blvd., Annapolis, MD 21401

ABBREVIATIONS

A	Artillery
admns	administer/administrix
AA	Anne Arundel
AL	Allegany
amt	Amount
Art	Artillery
atty	attorney
B	bugler
BA	Baltimore
bal	balance
Brig	Brigadier
Capt	Captain
CE	Cecil
Co	county
Col	Colonel
Corp	Corporal
D	Drummer (or dragoon?)
DO	Dorchester
ed	editor
Ens	Ensign
exec	executor
FK	Frederick
G	Gunner
Gen	General
HA	Harford
hus	husband
KT	Kent
lbs	pounds
Leg	Legion
Lieut	Lieutenant
Lt	Lieutenant
M	Matross
Maj	Major

mos	months
MT	Montgomery
Pvt	Private
Rec	Recruit (ed)
QM	Quartermaster
QMS	Quartermaster Sgt.
rec	recruit/recruited
rep (s)	representative(s)
Sgt	Sergeant
sh	shilling
SO	Somerset
sold	soldier
StM	St. Mary's
Surg	Surgeon
TA	Talbot
wid	widow
WO	Worcester

Standard Post Office abbreviations are used for names of states.

LIST OF OFFICERS AND SOLDIERS ENTITLED TO

LOTS WESTWARD OF FORT CUMBERLAND

ALLEGANY COUNTY

OFFICERS

Rank/Names   Lot Numbers Drawn

Rank/Names	Lot Numbers Drawn
Capt. George Armstrong	2367, 2368, 2395, 2396
Capt. Richard Anderson	3249, 3252, 3253, 3221
Lt. William Adams	2379, 2380. 2381, 2382
Capt. James Bruff	2711, 2712, 2713, 2714
Col. Peter Adams, 1st Regt.	2312, 2313, 2314, 2317
Maj. Archibald Anderson	2391, 2392, 2393, 2394
Chaplin James Armstrong	2589, 2590, 2591, 2592
Maj. Benjamin Brooks	2383, 2384, 2385, 2386
Capt. William Beatty	2421, 2422, 2423, 2424
Capt. Lloyd Beall	2773, 2774, 2767, 3310
Capt. Jacob Brice	3222, 3224, 3228, 3229
Maj. William Brown	1664, 1665, 1680, 1682
Capt. Joseph Burgess	2603, 2604, 2605, 2606
Maj. William Dent Beall	2489, 2490, 2583, 2584
Capt. William Bruce	2387, 2388, 2389, 2390
Capt. Perry Benson	1635, 1636, 1637, 1638
Lt. Thomas Boyd	2599, 2600, 2601, 2602
Capt. Michael Boyer	2268, 2269, 2270, 2271
Lt. Henry Baldwin	3200, 3201, 3198, 3199
Capt. John Sprigg Belt	3258, 3259, 3260, 3261
Capt. Richard Bird	1454, 1455, 1456, 1457

Lt. Joshua Burgess	2493, 2494, 2585, 2588
Lt. Samuel B. Beall	2337, 2338, 2349, 2350
Lt. Basil Burgess	3237, 3238, 3059, 3061
Lt. Henry Baker	2777, 2778, 2779, 2780
Lt. Thomas Beatty	1666, 1667, 1668, 1669
Lt. Malachai Bonham	2734, 2672, 2670, 2661
Lt. Jacques Bagues	1660, 1661, 1662, 1663
Capt. Charles Baltzell	2607, 2608, 2609, 2610
Lt. Joseph Britain	2498, 2499, 2573, 2574
Lt. John Brevett	3331, 3340, 3344, 3262
Lt. Joseph Cross	1683, 4128, 4129, 4130
Capt. Horatio Claggett	2954, 2955, 2956, 2957
Lt. Henry Chapman	2258, 2259, 2260, 2261
Lt. John Cary	2709, 2710, 2719, 2720
Surg. Gen. James Craig	2781, 2782, 2783, 2784
Lt. John Chever	2326, 2327, 2328, 2329
Lt. Jacob Crawford	2355, 2356, 2357, 2358
Lt. Edward Compton	3202, 3208, 3088, 3090
Lt. Henry Clements	2359, 2360, 2361, 2362
Capt. John Carlile	3191, 4140, 4141, 4142
Lt. John Carson	2280, 2282, 2284, 2285
Ens. Peter Cockey	2272, 2273, 2274, 2275
Capt. Charles Croxall	2363, 2364, 2365, 2366
Maj. John Davidson	2875, 2877, 2878, 2880
Capt. Rezin Davis	3345, 3346, 3347, 3348
Major Richard Dorsey	3600, 3601, 3602, 3849
Lt. Isaac Duvall	2293, 2281, 2283, 2134
Surg. Levin Denwood	2322, 2323, 2324, 2325
Lt. Robert Denny	2575. 2576, 2577, 2578
Capt. Henry Dobson	2189, 2190, 2069, 2070
Lt. Thomas A. Dyson	2620, 2622, 2623, 2624
Lt. Edward Duvall	2950, 2951, 3135, 3136
Lt. Walter Dyer	3203. 3204, 3205, 3209
Maj. John Deane	3234, 3051, 3053, 4151
Capt. Edward Dyer	3218, 3219, 3220, 3223
Lt. Richard Donovan	3611, 3612, 3613, 3614

Capt. Edward Edgerly	3607, 3608, 3609, 3610
Capt. James Ewing	3603, 3604, 3605, 3606
Surg. John L. Elbert	2621, 3246, 3248, 3251
Capt. Elijah Evans	3063, 3065, 3239, 3240
Lt. Samuel Edminston	3055, 3057, 3235, 3236
Lt. Col. Benjamin Ford, 6th Reg	3206, 3207, 3211, 3213
Lt. Col. Uriah Forrest, 1st Reg.	2715, 2716, 2717, 2718
Lt. Samuel Farmer	3266, 3333, 3334, 3337
Capt. Ebenezer Finley	2214, 2215, 2216, 2217
Lt. Benjamin Feckel	2660, 2664, 2668, 2669
Lt. Hezekiah Ford	3274, 3275, 3276, 3265
Brig. Gen. Mordecai Gist	2209, 2213, 2262, 2263
Capt. Edward Gale	2208, 2210, 2211, 2212
Col. John Gunby, 7th Reg.	2264, 2265, 2266, 2267
Capt. Jonathan Gibson	3242, 4145, 4146, 1679
Maj. Henry Gaither	2136, 2137, 2138, 2139
Capt. John Gassaway	3338, 3341, 3342, 3343
Capt. John Gale	2300, 2301, 2290, 2291
Lt. Henry Gassaway	2876, 2893, 2894, 2895
Lt. Richard Grace	2470, 2471, 2472, 2473
Capt. James Woolford Gray	2765, 2768, 2775, 2776
Lt. Benjamin Garnett	2059, 2115, 2117, 2152
Capt. John Gist	2225, 2226, 2227, 2228
Lt. Jacob Gromith	2736, 2737, 2738, 2739
Lt. James Gould	3137, 2964, 2966, 2968
Lt. William Goldsborough	3099, 4147, 4148, 1677
Lt. Nicholas Gassaway	3241, 4143, 4144, 1681
Lt. John Hardman	3079, 3080, 3081, 3082
Lt. John Hamilton	3214, 3215, 3216, 3217
Capt. George Hamilton	1570, 1571, 1572, 1573
Lt. Col. John Egar Howard, 5th Regt.	3243, 3244, 4149, 4138
Col. Josiah C. Hall, 4th Reg.	3083, 3084, 3085, 3086
Lt. Philip Hill	4136, 3271, 3272, 3273
Lt. Robert Hatkerston	2060, 2061, 2066, 2067
Lt. Samuel Hanson	2294, 2295, 2296, 2297
Lt. Arthur Harris	3305, 3306, 3307, 3313

Capt. John A. Hamilton	2482, 2483, 2484, 2485
Lt. Rignel Hillery	3193, 4134, 4139, 4132
Lt. Isaac Hanson	2611, 2612, 2613, 2614
Lt. Edward Hamilton	2286, 2287, 2288, 2289
Capt. George Handy	3267, 3268, 3269, 3270
Lt. Henry Hawkins	2118, 2119, 2298, 2299
Lt. William Hanson	2252, 2253, 2255, 2257
Surg. Ezekiel Haynie	2248, 2249, 2254, 2256
Capt. Thomas Hugon	2701, 2703, 2704, 2698
Sur. Mate Elisha Harrison	2343, 2344, 2345, 2346
Maj. David Hopkins	2351, 2352, 2353, 2354
Lt. John Hartshorn	2468, 2469, 2449, 2450
Maj. Henry Hardman	2997, 2998, 2999, 2883
Capt. Edward Hall	2302, 2303, 2315, 2316
Capt. Adam Hoops	2478, 2479, 2480, 2481
Capt. John Courts Jones	2702, 2705, 2708, 2699
Capt. John Jordan	3303, 3304, 3314, 2871
Lt. Adam Jamison	1565, 1670, 1672, 1673
Surg. William Kilty	2454, 2455, 2456, 2457
Capt. John Kilty	2140, 2141, 2142, 2128
Surg. Mate Samuel Y. Keene	2118, 2129, 2130, 2131
Maj. Thomas Lansdale	3210, 3212, 3231, 3233
Capt. David Lynn	2375, 2376, 2377, 2378
Maj. John Lynch	1578, 1579, 1580, 1632
Capt. James M. Lingan	4124, 4125, 4126, 4127
Lt. John Tolson Lowe	2593, 2594, 2496, 2497
Lt. John LeNashu	2132, 2133, 2321, 2320
Lt. John Lynn	2474, 2475, 2476, 2477
Capt. Thomas H. Luckett	2428, 2430, 2434, 2435
Capt. William Lamar	2443, 2444, 2447, 2427
Capt. David Luckett	2671, 2673, 2674, 2675
Capt. Samuel McPherson	1498, 1671, 1676, 1678
Capt. John Mitchell	3194, 3195, 3196, 3197
Capt. John Morris	2062, 2063, 2064, 2065
Capt. Thomas Mason	2058, 2071, 2072, 2079
Capt. Nicholas Mangers	2124, 2125, 2126, 2078

Capt. Joseph Marberry	2073, 2074, 2076, 2077
Lt. Mark McPherson	2276, 2277, 2278, 2279
Capt. Christian Myres	2075, 2114, 2116, 2119
Capt. James McFaden	2676, 2677, 2680, 2681
Capt. Walker Muse	2461, 2462, 2491, 2480
Lt. John McCoy	2700, 2689, 2688, 2697
Lt. Zedikaih Moore	2690, 2685, 2684, 2682
Ens. Caleb Mason	2595, 2596, 2597, 2598
Lt. Lawrence Myers	2465, 2466, 2492, 2495
Lt. David Morgan	2304, 2306, 2308, 2309
Capt. Jacob Norris	2582, 2586, 2587, 2683
Lt. Roger Nelson	2845, 2847, 2849, 2868
Lt. John Nelson	2336, 2337, 2338, 2436
Capt. Edward Oldham	3302, 3279, 3280, 4119
Lt. Thomas Price	2881, 2882, 2888, 2889
Capt. Edward Prall	1574, 1575, 1576, 1577
Capt. Benjamin Price	2110, 2111, 2143, 2145
Lt. William Pendergast	2112, 2113, 2135, 2292
Surg. Richard Pindell	4120, 4121, 4122, 4123
Col. Nathaniel Ramsey, 30th Reg.	2127, 2144, 2146, 2147
Capt. Chris'r. Richmond	2740, 2741, 2742, 2743
Capt. William Riely	1457, 1458, 1459, 1460
Capt. Philip Reed	2096, 2097, 2098, 2099
Maj. Alexander Roxburgh	3230, 3232, 3226, 3227
Lt. Isaac Rawlings	3184, 3185, 3186, 3187
Maj. John Rudloph	3225, 3245, 3247, 3250
Lt. John Rutledge	2691, 2692, 2693, 2694
Lt. Jacob Raybolt	2846, 2848, 2850, 2896
Capt. Francis Revely	2728, 2729, 2730, 2731
Lt. Nicholas Ricketts	2870, 2872, 2873, 2874
Lt. Thomas Rouse	2401, 2402, 2403, 2404
Lt. William Raison	2405, 2406, 2407, 2408
Capt. Michael Rudolph	2764, 2766, 2726, 2727
Maj. Gen. William Smallwood	2409, 2410, 2411, 2412
Col. John H. Stone, 1st Reg.	2399, 2400, 2334, 2335
Maj. Alex H. Smith	2721, 2722, 2724, 2725

Maj. Jonathan Sellman	3893, 3894, 3895, 2525
Capt. Edward Spurrier	2987, 2988, 2989, 2990
Capt. John Smith, 3rd Reg.	2958, 2959, 2961, 2963
Capt. James Somerville	2960, 2962, 2945, 2949
Capt. Clement Skerrilt	2723, 2732, 2733, 2735
Lt. Col. John Stewart	2756, 2757, 2758, 2759
Lt. John Sears	2748, 2749, 2750, 2751
Maj. John Swan	2706, 2707, 2695, 2696
Lt. William Smoot	3315, 3316, 2867, 2869
Surg. Mate, Alex. Smith	2975, 2976, 2977, 2978
Lt. Martin Shugart	2983, 2984, 2985, 2986
Capt. John Smith, 6th Reg.	2969, 2971, 2973, 2974
Lt. Edward M. Smith	2441, 2442, 2460, 2463
Capt. James Smith, Artillery	2970, 2972, 3138, 3139
Lt. William T. Stoddert	2413, 2414, 2415, 2416
Capt. Joseph Smith	4131, 4133, 4135, 4137
Ens. Jacob Shoemaker	3188, 3189, 3190, 3192
Maj. Alexander Trueman	2617, 3263, 3264, 3619
Lt. Col. Edward Tillard	1566, 1567, 1568, 1569
Capt. Adomson Tannehill	2371, 2372, 2373, 2374
Lt. Josiah Tanehill	2887, 2890, 2891, 2892
Lt. John Trueman	3180, 3181, 3182, 3183
Capt. Lilburn Williams	2615, 2616, 2618, 2619
Brig,. Gen. Otho Holland Williams	2687, 2686, 2678, 2679
Col. Thomas Wooford	1656, 1657, 1658, 1659
Capt. William Wilmot	2752, 2753, 2754, 2755
Lt. William Woolford	2979, 2980, 2981, 2982
Capt. Richard Waters	2944, 2946, 2947, 2879
Lt. Col. Levin Winder	2884, 2885, 2886, 2996
Capt. James Winchester	2760, 2761, 2762, 2763
Lt. Robert Wilmot	2744, 2745, 2746, 2747
Surg. Mate Gerard Wood	2148, 2149, 2150, 2151
Lt. Francis Ware	2952, 2953, 2965, 2967
Surg. Mate William Wate	2339, 2340, 2341, 2342
Lt. Gassaway Watkins	2244, 2245, 2246, 2247
Surg. Walter Warfield	2837, 2842, 2843, 2844

Lt. Nathan Wright	2092, 2093, 2094, 2095
Lt. Col. Ludowick Weltner, Ger. Reg.	3254, 3255, 3256, 3257
Lt. George Winchester	2451, 2452, 2453, 2448
Capt. Nathan Williams	2330, 2331, 2332, 2332 [sic]
Lt. Young Wilkinson	2305, 2307, 2310, 2311
Lt. Basil Waring	2445, 2446, 2464, 2467
Lt. William Towson	2431, 2432, 2433, 2429
Capt. Peregrine Fitzhugh	3335, 3336, 3332, 3339
Lt. William Fitzhugh	2940, 2941, 2942, 2943
Lt. William Murdoch	2417, 2418, 2419, 2420

SOLDIERS

Names	Rank	Regiment	Lot Number Drawn
Adam Adams	Pvt.	1	1876
Ignatius Adams	Pvt.	1	1163
John Alvey	Pvt.	2	2033
John Appleby	Pvt.	3	1131
Daniel Anderson	Pvt.	4	1318
James Allen	Pvt.	5	27
Thomas Ayres	Pvt.	5	1168
Emanuel Allen	Pvt.	5	1160
John Andrews	Pvt.	5	2537
William Ayhern	Pvt.	6	3174
John Armstrong, 1st	Pvt.	2	1956
John Ashmore	Pvt.	7	3121
George Abbott	Pvt.	2	2544
Cuthbert Able	Sgt.	7	1146
John Adams	Corp	3	1117

Name	Rank	Unit	Number
Thomas Arthur	Pvt	State	2528
John Auber	Pvt	State	2520
John Ashbury	Pvt	State	2571
John Armstrong, 2nd	Pvt	6	1901
Harris Austin	Pvt	5	138
Josiah Alvey	Pvt	1	2034
Jacob Adams	Pvt	Rawlings	4059
John Adams, 2nd	Pvt	State	1748
John Anderson, 1st	Pvt	3	62
Peregrine Asque	M.	Artillery	930
William Allen	M.	Artillery	1949
Thomas Adams	Pvt	3	876
James Ashley	Pvt	German	950
William Absolum	Pvt	Recruit 81	
Travers Alvey	Pvt	3	
Nathan Aldridge	Pvt	German	
John Anderson	Pvt	7	
Henry Austin	Pvt	2	
Thomas Aspin	Pvt	2	
Frederick Ayres	Pvt	6	
Thomas Allison	Pvt	1	
Michael Anderson	Pvt	Hazen's	
Barnet Alley	Pvt	Lee's Legion	
James Arrants	Pvt	Lee's Legion	
James Addy or Eddy	Pvt	2	
Thomas G. Alvey	Pvt	3	
Daniel Basil	fifer	1	1882
John Baker	Pvt	1	2545
George Bateman	Pvt	1	1825
John Brookbank	Pvt	1	3118
Levi Burk	Pvt	2	1256
Thomas Buckley	Sgt	2	1330
William Brookes	Pvt	2	1992
Barruch Butt	Pvt	2	1970
Thomas Butt	Pvt	2	4036
Edward Butt	Pvt	2	1818

Name	Rank		Number
Frederick Bennett	Fifer	2	2040
Solomon Brittenham	Pvt.	2	131
Levy Button	Pvt.	2	1893
Levin Bramble	Pvt.	2	3129
John Blades	Pvt.	2	585
Thomas Brown	Corp	3	951
John Brown, 1st	Pvt.	3	1948
Richard Butler	Pvt	3	1169
John Barrett	Pvt.	3	1142
Basil Brown	Pvt.	3	1780
George Brown	Pvt.	3	2084
Zachariah Burch	Pvt	3	91
Leonard Bean	Corp	3	1827
Gabriel Brand	Pvt.	3	471
John Bean	Pvt	3	814
Thomas Bird	Pvt.	3	3015
Benjamin Boyd	Pvt.	3	2027
John Blair, 2nd	Pvt.	3	997
Peter Bochard	Pvt	3	873
Thomas Bailey	Pvt.	3	1043
John Buckley	Pvt.	3	872
Joshua Barret	Sgt.	4	101
George Bradley	Corp.	4	1407
Peter Bowler	Pvt.	4	194
Joshua Batchely	Pvt.	4	1381
Robert Bowen	Fifer	4	2535
Philip Bailey	Pvt.	4	1037
John Beach	Drummer	4	1148
John Buchanan	Drummer	1	2025
Daniel Buckley	Pvt	2	1757
James Biass	Pvt.	3	1139
John Barnett	Pvt.	5	1026
Perry Burtham	Pvt.	5	1072
John Brent	Fifer	5	1411
George Blackham	Pvt	5	3
James Barron	Pvt	5	159

James Bailey	Pvt	5	2000
Abram Bowen	Pvt.	5	1940
John Bantham	Pvt	5	41
Solomon Barrett	Pvt.	5	1797
James Burk, 1st	Pvt.	6	1771
John Brown, 2nd	Sgt.	6	1059
Henry Billop	Pvt.	6	1275
Thomas Bear	Pvt.	6	1849
George Bumgardner	Pvt.	6	2035
Benjamin Burch, 2nd	Corp	6	1556
Thomas Brady	Pvt.	6	1464
Joseph Blaize	Pvt.	7	2002
Joseph Botts	Pvt.	7	986
Moses Barney	Pvt.	7	1360
Richard Boone	Pvt.	7	3120
Joshua Brown	Pvt.	7	1881
Joseph Burgess	Pvt.	7	1603
Humphrey Beckett	Sgt.	7	1086
Laurence Brannan	Sgt.	7	1581
George Brown	Pvt.	7	2541
George Buck	Pvt.	7	182
Abijah Buxton	Pvt	1	1875
Jesse Barnett	Fifer	7	1489
Thomas Bowser	Pvt.	5	1935
James Baber	Pvt.	State	4111
Daniel Bulger	Pvt.	7	4113
Jesse Boswell	Corp	State	1831
Joseph Barton	Pvt.	State	3027
Martin Bowles	Pvt	7	....
John Brewer	Pvt.	State	....
John Branson	Pvt.	State	....
Jeremiah Brown	Pvt.	State	....
Richard Biddle	Pvt.	State	....
James Bigwood	Pvt	State	....
Peter Bushell	Pvt	4	....
Thomas Baker	Pvt	State	....

James Balip [Baliss?]	Pvt	State	...
John Berriman (Banneman)	Pvt	4	.....
James Brannan	Pvt	2	1057
John Brian	Pvt	State	1112
John Biggs	Pvt	State	1859
Jacob Blake	Pvt	State	1785
John Brown, 3rd	Corp	Rawling's	75
Benjamin Burch	Sgt	Rawlings	1123
George Bough	Pvt	German	1134
Samuel Boswell	Pvt	German	2521
William Batten	Pvt	Rawlings	1351
Zachariah Berry	Pvt	Rawlings	2547
James Bryan	Pvt	1	3166
John Bayley, 1sr	Pvt	3	1147
William Burgess	Pvt	3	3001
George Belfast	Pvt.	Rec. 81	1051
Charles Buckliss	Pvt	State	3044
John Brady	Sgt	State	1416
James Barrow	Pvt	State	888
Thomas Baxter	Pvt	State	936
James Blewer	Pvt	3	1369
John Butcher	Pvt	3	188
Nathan Bateman	Pvt	5	2016
John Bennet	Pvt	State	63
Joseph Burch	Pvt	2	1089
Thomas Bishop	Pvt	2	1127
William Braithwait	Pvt	2	4107
Richard Blansford	Pvt	2	1076
Thomas Brown	Sgt	Art	1904
Isaac Burton	M	Art	2549
Thomas Brown	M	Art	1199
Edward Berry	M	Art	4104
Thomas Bowler	M	Art	881
John Brady	M	Art	1510
Thomas Barber	M	Art.	1170
Thomas Barclay or Bartley	Pvt	3	1905

William Bruff	Pvt	7	1782
David Bramble	Pvt	2	1888
John Burnes	Pvt	Rec. 81	2539
Benjamin Bough	Pvt	Rec. 81	57
John Boudy	Pvt	Rec. 81	1561
John Boody	Pvt.	Rec. 81	891
John Britton	Pvt	Rec. 81	26
John Briley	Pvt	Rec. 81	103
Benjamin Belcher	Pvt	Rec. 81	1846
Thomas Burch, 2nd	Pvt.	Rec. 81	1149
Nathaniel Barley	Pvt	Rec. 81	393
Andrew Bramble	Pvt	Rec. 81	1698
John Baxter	Pvt	Rec. 81	3058
James Bowen	Pvt	Rec. 81	1185
Joel Baker	Pvt	7	1177
William Brady	Pvt	Rec. 81	992
John Blair, 1st	Pvt	7	3023
George Bowers	Pvt	6	3152
James Bayley	Drummer	3	993
James Berry	M	Art	1703
Robert Britt	Pvt	1	1052
Luke Burnes	Pvt	1	4029
William Bowles	Pvt	2	4066
Daniel Boyles	Pvt	2	1963
Ezekiel Burnes	Pvt	2	989
John Burnes	Pvt.	2	1465
Zachariah Butts	Pvt	2	1934
Charles Byrn	Pvt	2	1903
James Banny	Pvt	3	1181
Hugh Burns	Pvt	3	1154
Thomas Buttery	Pvt	3	1536
William Bolton	Pvt	3	1172
James Brown	Pvt.	5	1742
John Benny	Pvt.	5	4096
Alexander Beck	Pvt	5	887
Michael Burns	Pvt	5	1537

Hugh Batton	Pvt	6	1981
Robert Body	Fifer	6	3008
John Brown	Pvt	6	3064
James Boyle	Pvt	6	1918
Harvey Burnes	Pvt	Hazen's	1115
John Batton	Pvt	Hazen's	29
William Brown	Pvt	Hazen's	4103
Nehemiah Barns	Pvt	Hazen's	1221
Richard Basset	Pvt	Lee's Legion	1763
George Bowe	Pvt	Lee's Legion	1267
John Bennet	Pvt.	Lee's Legion	434
James Brown	Pvt	Lee's Legion	1207
Thomas Broome	Pvt	Lee's Legion	1840
William Bright	Pvt	4	953
Robert Barnet	Pvt	German	1740
William Clary	Pvt	1	4158
Thomas Buttery	Pvt	3	1536
William Bolton	Pvt	3	1172
James Brown	Pvt	5	1742
John Benny	Pvt	5	4096
Alexander Beck	Pvt	5	887
Michael Burns	Pvt	5	1537
Hugh Batton	Pvt	6	1981
Robert Body	Fifer	6	3008
John Brown	Pvt	6	3064
James Boyle	Pvt	6	1918
Harvey Burnes	Pvt	Hazen's	1115
John Batton	Pvt	Hazen's	29
William Brown	Pvt	Hazen's	4103
Nehemiah Barns	Pvt	Hazen's	1221
Richard Basset	Pvt	Lee's Legion	1763
George Bowe	Pvt	Lee's Legion	1267
John Bennet	Pvt	Lee's Legion	434
James Brown	Pvt	Lee's Legion	1207
Thomas Broome	Pvt	Lee's Legion	1840
William Bright	Pvt	4	953

Name	Rank	Co.	No.
Robert Barnet	Pvt	German	1740
William Clary	Pvt	1	4153
David Caile	Pvt	1	2397
John Carroll, 1st	Pvt	1	2504
James Collard	Fifer	1	4044
Wm. Clements, 2nd	Pvt	1	1182
Michael Cole	Pvt	1	1178
Thomas Campher	Pvt	2	493
Patrick Cavenaugh	State	2	1266
William Cato	Pvt	2	1675
Hugh Cain	Pvt	2	1063
David Conner, 1st	Pvt	2	1092
Morris Citizen	Pvt	2	1095
William Chatland	Pvt	2	1922
William Cutler	Pvt	2	1910
John Camphen	Pvt	2	2369
Hamton Coursey	Pvt	2	821
William Conner, 1st	Pvt	2	193
George Childs	Corp	3	79
Daniel Claney	Pvt	3	1832
John Craig	Pvt	3	3094
Barton Cecil	Pvt	3	90
Charles Clements	Pvt	3	4165
Luke Carter	Pvt	3	4152
John Claggett	Pvt	3	3161
Thomas Clark, 1st	Pvt	3	123
Heze. Carr	Drummer	3	472
John Courts	Pvt	3	1604
Michael Clark	Pvt	4	1931
John Colin	Sgt	4	4157
Thomas B. Clements	Pvt	Rec. 81	1911
William Cartro, 2nd	Pvt	4	1135
Emanuel Cathagone	Pvt	4	1020
Abram Catchsides	Pvt	4	4022
Thomas Clinton	Fifer	4	1108
Michael Callhan	Pvt	4	158

Aseph Colegate	Pvt	4	1919
Andrew Crummy	Pvt	2	1132
John Carr	Pvt	3	911
Robert Cornick	Pvt	5	191
John Carroll, 2nd	Pvt	5	459
Charles Crouch	Sgt	5	1028
Augustine Cann	Pvt	5	1833
Thomas Carney	Pvt	5	1067
Michael Claney	Fifer	5	1066
Thomas Cahoe, Sr.	Pvt	6	4100
Thomas Cahoe, Jr	Fifer	6	4109
Benjamin Cleaver	Pvt	6	1417
Charistopher Cusick	Pvt	6	1006
Robt. Callahan or Clemmahan	Pvt	6	1805
William Cook	Pvt	6	1175
William Craile	Pvt	7	962
Darby Crowley	Pvt	7	474
John Cheshire	Sgt	7	475
William Casey	Pvt	7	461
Adam Crow	Pvt	Rec. 81	1704
William Cummins	Pvt	7	1446
Aquilla Chitham	Pvt	7	1562
Owen Carey	Corp	7	21
Ignatius Compton	Pvt	7	1032
James Curren	Pvt	7	168
Stephen Carr	Pvt	7	162
Edward Claney	Fifer	7	167
John Cochran	Pvt	7	166
William Collis	Sgt	State	1208
Jonathan Chubb	Pvt	State	3119
William Chapman	Pvt	State	1402
William Crook	Pvt	State	3035
William Cox	Pvt	State	909
Henry Craine	Pvt	State	1033
George Clarke	Pvt	State	808
Thomas Cooper	Pvt	State	1487

Name	Rank	Unit	Number
Bennet H. Clements	Pvt	State	1920
James Casey	Pvt	State	1913
Lewis Cunningham	Pvt	State	1520
Calothile Carmile	Pvt	State	1755
David Crady	Fifer	State	1802
Michael Casner	Pvt	State	1058
Samuel Callahan	Pvt.	3	1753
John Cooper, 1st	Pvt	State	1752
George Craigs	Pvt	4	3164
Dominick Coins	Pvt	6	906
Benjamin Cole	Pvt	German	477
John Connelly, 1st	Pvt	Gist's	3033
Isham Coleman	Pvt	State	1467
William Carter, 1st	Pvt	State	1497
James Crozier	Pvt	State	2570
Peter Carberry	Pvt	State	56
Samuel Chapple	Pvt	State	1982
Michael Curtis	Pvt	State	176
William Clements, 1st	Pvt	5	1790
Kindall Cobb	Pvt	Rec. 81	4155
Thomas Cannady	Pvt	3	1149
Valentine Clapper	Pvt	State	4052
Charles Cooper	Pvt	2	1167
John Carson	Sgt	Rec. 81	297
Elijah Cockendall	Corp	Rawling's	1506
John Crosby, 1st	Pvt	4	278
Dennis Cragan	Pvt	1	340
Joseph Cooley	Pvt	1	1282
Thomas Craig	Sgt	Rawling's	960
Edward Cosgrove	Pvt	1	298
John Clancey, 2nd	Corp	1	458
James Crawford	Pvt	3	1214
William Civill	Pvt	5	1294
Timothy Cahill	Pvt	German	23
Jacob Carnant	Pvt	7	921
John Carter	Pvt	State	923

Owen Coffeild	Pvt	Grayson's	924
George Collins	Pvt	3	4144
Bryan Carroll	Pvt	2	3126
Michael Coyle	Pvt	6	479
Edward Cain	Pvt	4	1104
Joseph Crouch	Pvt	3	1035
Thomas Cardiff	Pvt	3	973
John Cole	Pvt	Rec. 81	1150
Jacob Collins	Pvt	2	902
James Chambers	Pvt	Rec. 81	183
John Collins	Pvt	Rec. 81	1130
Thomas Clarke	Pvt	Rec. 81	1155
Thomas Condrum	Corp	Artillery	1126
Arthur Carns	Corp	Artillery	1068
Hugh Chaplin	M	Artillery	1861
Timothy Connelly	Sgt	Artillery	1860
William Cornwell	Sgt	Artillery	857
Samuel Carter	Sgt	Artillery	1950
John Clark	Gunner	Artillery	432
Michael Conner	M	Artillery	1307
John Compton	M	Artillery	1483
Robert Campbell	M	Artillery	4156
James Clarke	M	Artillery	858
John Curl	Pvt	State	1044
John Cleverdence	Pvt	Rec. 81	42
Arthur Coffin	Pvt	Rec. 81	105
Josua Cox	Pvt	Rec. 81	47
Edward Chamber	Pvt	Rec. 81	979
James Chard	Pvt	Rec. 81	1159
Jame Cochran	Pvt	Rec. 81	925
John Cannon	Pvt	Rec. 81	1491
Thomas Compton	Pvt	Rec. 81	1194
James Collins	Sgt	7	1607
William Cork	Pvt	Rec. 81	1631
George Carney	Pvt	Rec. 81	1060
Kobert Carnes	Pvt	Rec. 81	1252

Matthias Cyphart	Pvt	Rec. 81	1418
James Clements	Pvt	Rec. 81	1593
William Coe	Pvt	Rec. 81	1595
James Crasbury	Pvt	Rec. 81	800
William Cann	Pvt	Rec. 81	1295
Zachariah Clark	Fifer	3	1983
Samuel Clark	Pvt	7	1425
Robert Campbell	Pvt	Rec. 81	1218
John Campbell, 2nd	Pvt	Rec. 81	1109
John Connelly, 2nd	Pvt	Gist's	1812
William Coursey	Pvt.	Rec. 81	1626
Patrick Conner	Pvt	2	3078
Peter Casey	Pvt	7	1118
Michael Carr's Admns			457
Benajamin Carns	Pvt	2	1866
John Curritt	Pvt	1	4110
Thomas Chapman	Pvt	1	1473
Samuel Chinn	Pvt	1	3004
Robert Cooley	Pvt	1	1300
John Cole	Pvt	2	864
John Cernish	Pvt	2	1245
Joseph Cullamine	Pvt	3	1298
Bennet Cheser	Pvt	3	1343
Barney Cassaday	Pvt	3	53
John Cox	Pvt	3	189
Justinian Carter	Pvt	3	38
William Collier	Pvt	3	52
William Cougleton	Pvt	4	1490
Simon Chappoik	Pvt	4	946
James Conner	Pvt	5	1813
John Caves	Pvt	5	1907
Michael Claney, Sr	Sgt	5	1789
Peter Carwell	Sgt	6	1102
Michael Corr	Sgt	6	414
John Crozier	Sgt	6	412
Peter Cunningham	Pvt	7	82

Name	Rank	Unit	No.
John Clarke	Pvt	7	25
Richard Clarke	Pvt	7	342
Nicholas Campbell	Pvt	7	3171
Hugh Connelly	Pvt	Hazen's	436
John Craig	Pvt	Hazen's	3172
John Coomy (Kumy)	Pvt	Hazen's	4031
John Collins	Pvt	Hazen's	437
Jesse Crasbie	Pvt	Lee's Leg	438
Robert Crouch	Pvt	Lee's Leg	1038
William or Benjn. Chestnut	Pvt	Lee's Leg	846
Charles Dawkins	Sgt	1	156
Dennis Dunning	Drummer	1	445
John Dixon, 1st	Pvt	1	1985
Francis Dunar	Pvt	1	2572
William Dortch	Pvt	1	1244
Henry Dixon	Pvt	1	497
John Denson	Pvt	2	867
George Dixon	Pvt	2	84
William Dixon	Pvt	3	1082
John Dyer	Pvt	3	1674
Aquilla Deaver	Pvt	3	4045
Luke Dempsey	Pvt	3	1354
Thomas Drudge	Pvt	3	1505
John Donovan	Pvt	4	121
William Downes	Pvt	4	130
Thomas Doyle	Pvt	4	1628
Peter Degazoon	Pvt	4	454
James Daffin	Corp	4	485
Edmund Dougherty	Sgt	4	1714
Francis Dunnington	Pvt	2	1692
James Doyle	Pvt	5	1543
John Duhague	Pvt	5	1508
John Downey	Pvt	5	1707
Elijah Deane	Pvt	5	212
Robert Davis	Pvt	6	1717
Richard Duvall	Pvt	6	1550

Name	Rank	Unit	Number
Patrick Doran	Sgt	6	1481
John Denson	Drummer	6	1909
James Devereux	Sgt	6	1504
George Devit	Pvt	7	480
Robert Duncan	Pvt	7	1527
Samuel Davis, 1st	Sgt	7	1716
Samuel Denny	Pvt	7	1232
James Dyer, 1st	Pvt	3	1602
John Delanaway	Pvt	6	1525
Matthias Dyche	Pvt	6	1627
John Deakins	Pvt	State	1689
Edward Dominick	Pvt	State	1954
Joseph Donohoe	Pvt	State	1858
James Davidson	Pvt	1	443
William Deaver	Pvt	3	1697
James Dure	Pvt	5	1161
William Devine	Pvt	State	1848
James Dyer, 2nd	Pvt	German	1800
John Donagan	Pvt	State	1189
William Dunnington or Derrington	Pvt	3	114
Joseph Deford	Pvt	5	1027
Alexander Downey	Pvt	5	1011
Richard Dixon	Pvt	7	1085
Francis Duvist	Pvt	Rawlings	466
James Dowden	Pvt	Rawlings	1583
Butoc Deveaux	Pvt	1	4038
John Dent	Pvt	3	4039
John Dove	Sgt	7	1941
Beryer Dominick	Pvt	6	1197
James Dennison	Pvt	Rawlings	1736
Richard Downs	Pvt	7	1474
Pearce Deakin	Pvt	Rawlings	1761
William Day	Pvt	State	1921
James Davidson	Pvt	1	1727
Thomas Dutton	Pvt		1788

Charles Davis	Pvt	Rec. 81	397
William Davis	M	Art	1255
William Dixon	B	Art	3130
Peter Davis	D	Art	427
John Davis, 1st	Pvt	Rec. 81	293
William Dawson	Pvt	Rec. 81	273
Barnably Dohorty	Pvt	5	314
Jacob Duders	Pvt	Rec. 81	241
Terrence Duffy	Pvt	6	428
John Deane	Pvt	Rec. 81	1121
John Dobson	Pvt	Rec. 81	490
James Drian	Pvt.	Rec. 81	1235
Thomas Duffy	Pvt	Rec. 81	812
Thomas Davis, 1st	Pvt	Rec. 81	1625
Abram Dugan	Pvt	Rec. 81	963
Thomas Dickison	Pvt	Rec. 81	338
Charles Deane	Pvt	Rec. 81	1957
Richard Dolvin	Pvt	Rec. 81	324
Richard Dunby	Pvt	Rec. 81	426
James Dawson	Pvt	Rec. 81	240
Timothy Donovan	M	Art	272
Thomas Dutton's Admns	Pvt	1	292
Thomas Daley	Pvt	2	317
John Davis	Pvt	3	337
John Davis of Bailey's Co.	Pvt	3	364
James Douglas of Bailey's Co	Pvt	3	385
James Divine of Bailey's Co	Pvt	4	406
Michael Duffy	Pvt	4	1953
John Deford	Pvt	5	1210
Patrick Durgan	Pvt	5	407
Peter Dunston	Pvt	6	1421
Thomas Disharoon	Pvt	7	1426
George Dice (or Dias)	Pvt	5	467
Francis Duffy	S	Rec. 81	1094
Jeremiah Driskill	Pvt	4	1524
George Dyer	Pvt	5	1600

John Davis	Pvt	Rec. 81	1119
Patrick Dennsion	Pvt	4	448
William Deakins	Pvt	Hazen's	1588
Thomas Deavor	Pvt	Hazen's	1427
William Douley	Pvt	Hazen's	446
William Dowdle	Pvt	Lee's Leg	1549
Joseph Deale	Pvt	Art	386
Michael Dowlan	Pvt	N. Gist's	1712
Henry Evans	Pvt	Rec. 81	1539
Edward Ellicott	Pvt	1	1432
Peregrine Evans	Sgt	2	439
Bartholomew Esom	Corp	2	949
Michael Ellis	Fifer	2	1434
Thomas Evans, 2nd	Pvt	3	1705
Thomas Ellicott, 2nd	Pvt	3	1433
William Ellis	Pvt	4	1589
Edward Evans, 1st	Pvt	4	972
William Evans	Pvt	4	1204
Thomas Edwards	Sgt	4	1428
Jarvis Eccleston	Pvt	5	239
Joseph Ellicott	Pvt	6	1685
George Elms	Fife Maj	6	1231
John Ellicott, 1st	Pvt	6	382
Edward Evans, 2nd	Sgt	State	1271
William Elkins	Pvt	State	365
Thomas Ellis, 1st	Pvt	State	969
Enork Ennis	Pvt	State	850
Leonard Ennis	Pvt	State	1236
John Ennis	Pvt.	State	1249
John Edwards	Pvt	Rec. 81	465
Peter Edquidowney	Pvt	Rec. 81	494
James Evans	Pvt	Rec. 81	316
Thomas Elliott, 1st	Pvt	Rec. 81	817
Samuel Evans	Corp	Rec. 81	1738
Thomas Evans, 1st	Pvt	Rec. 81	4041
Heathesat Edwards	Pvt	Rec. 81	1794

Emanuel Ebbs	Pvt	Gist's	1750
Euel Evans	Pvt	State	1883
Thomas Ellison	Pvt	1	1863
John Edwards	Sgt	3	391
Richard Ellis' Admns		5	449
Frederick Eyen		Art	441
John Evans	M	Art	1553
Benjamin Evans		6	1310
John Etheridge		6	1691
Richard Ellison	Pvt	7	901
James Ervine	Pvt	Rec. 81	1304
Nicholas Elliott	Pvt	Rec. 81	932
James Edes	Pvt	Hazen's	220
Edward Ervine	Pvt		255
Jacob Flora	Pvt	1	1083
Francis Fairbrother	Pvt	1	34
John Franeway	Pvt	1	1898
Stephen Fresh	Pvt	1	20
Joseph Fowler	Pvt	1	914
William Fisher	Pvt	1	844
Jonathan Fowler	Pvt	1	328
George Fellason or Fenlayson	Pvt	2	213
Henry Fisher, 2nd	Pvt	German	1423
James Farrel	Pvt	2	341
James Fitzjerald	Pvt	2	16
Francis Freeman	Pvt	2	1424
John Ferguson	Pvt	2	1781
Edward Furriner	Pvt	3	2501
James Forster	Pvt	3	1845
Alexander Francis	Pvt	3	1841
Richard Freeman	Pvt	3	164
William R. Franklin	Pvt	3	1077
John Farrell	Pvt	3	1750
Richard Farraby	Pvt	4	1141
Frederick Flinon	Pvt	4	1042
Stafford Fosdale	Pvt	4	3098

Peter Fountain	Pvt	4	2486
Banjamin Folliot	Pvt	4	153
Rigby Foster	Pvt	5	947
William Foreman	Sgt	5	3113
William Farrell	Drummer	5	148
John Fulham	Pvt	5	3062
Edward Flowers	Pvt	5	810
Mark Forster	Pvt	5	1284
Benjamin Fitzgerald	Sgt	7	172
Absolum Fardo	Pvt	7	22
John M. Funner	Pvt	7	3165
Doras Filmont	Pvt	7	1062
Nicholas Fitzgerald	Pvt	7	1871
Moses Forster	Pvt	7	2024
Samuel Filson	Sgt	7	3131
Stephen Fluhart	Sgt	1 & 7	3097
Dennis Flannigan	M	Art	3178
Emanuel Farara	Pvt	State	174
Philip Fisher	Pvt	State	1339
John Folling	Pvt	State	1924
Robert Farrel	Pvt	State	1211
Jeremiah French	Pvt	State	896
Philip Fitzpatrick	Pvt	State	905
Charles Fitzgerald	Pvt	State	971
William Fitzgerald	Pvt	State	1932
John Frawney	Pvt	State	1329
John Finley	Sgt	Rec. 81	4159
Roger Folger	Pvt	Rec. 81	1328
Peter French	Corp	Rec. 81	965
Thomas Foxall	Pvt	Rec. 81	893
Edward Finchham	Pvt	Rec. 81	1816
John Fosset	Pvt	Rec. 81	345
Walter Farrel	Pvt	Rec. 81	815
David Foxall	Pvt	Rec. 81	128
Stephen Fennell	Pvt	State	1049
George Ford	Pvt	5	1162

Name	Rank	Unit	Number
John Fulford	Pvt	State	1737
George Fields	Sgt	3	1003
Robert Firth	Sgt	Rawling's	938
Thomas Flemming	Sgt	Rawling's	994
Joseph Fisher	Sgt	Rec. 81	2085
John Fennel	Sgt	German	933
Charles Fulham	Corp	German	2088
John Franklin	Pvt	German	4097
Joseph Folliot	Pvt	4	55
Thomas Frumley	Pvt	5	4105
Henry Fisher, 1st	Pvt	Rec. 81	2001
William Fairburn	Pvt	3	3167
Jeremiah Fitzjerald	Pvt	7	455
Richard Fenwick	pvt	4	1729
Andrew Fernan	Pvt	3	1452
Thomas Fanning	M	Art	1019
John Fitzjerald, Jr	M	Art	907
Benjamin Freshwater		1	3009
Robert Ford	Sgt	4	1373
John Fairbank		5	1408
William Fountain		5	1530
Edward Fennel		7	1730
Massey Fluart		Hazen's	1995
Samuel Frazier		Hazen's	2029
James Flood		Hazen's	1974
William French		Lee's Leg	1196
Edmund Flowers		5	3160
Robert Freemoutt		3	1041
James Flack	Sgt	6	1074
Peter Farrell	Corp	State	462
Benjamin Gray	Sgt	7	1973
Amos Gree	Pvt	1	3054
Abraham Garcena	Pvt	1	899
Samuel Green	Pvt	1	1972
John Green, 1st	Pvt	1	2018
William Griffin	Fifer	1	1997

Thomas Glover	Pvt	1	1978
Andrew Garnet	Fifer	2	3123
William Gould	Pvt	2	1923
Mark Griffin	Pvt	2	1959
Nathan Griffin	Pvt	2	822
Rubin Goostry	Pvt	2	1333
Henry Green	Pvt	2	1340
Thomas Gossage	Pvt	2	1205
Anthony Geohagan	Drummer	3	1563
Jesse Grace	Drummer	3	1229
John Gibson	Pvt	3	811
Isaac Green	Pvt	3	33
William Glascow	Pvt	3	1258
Charles Goldsborough	Pvt	3	1828
John Gordon, 1st	Pvt	3	1253
William Gates	Drummer	3	1610
John Goddard	Pvt	3	3107
Hugh Gainer	Pvt	3	210
James Garth	Pvt	4	415
John Gwynn	Sgt	4	1309
James Gray, 1st	Pvt	4	1176
John Gorman, 1st	Pvt	4	3032
Thomas Gillon	Pvt	5	1824
Henry Gilby	Pvt	5	3072
Abraham Gamble	Pvt	5	3010
James Greenwood	Drummer	6	1996
Moses Grahame	Pvt	6	3056
Isaac Graves	Pvt	6	201
Edward Garish	Pvt	6	1515
Paul Grenard	Pvt	6	100
Richard Gee	Pvt	7	1762
Samuel Gerry	Pvt	7	484
Joseph Gordon	Pvt	7	1928
Henry Goldsborough	Pvt	3	4049
John Gordon, 2nd	Pvt.	Rawlings	1855
William Glory	Pvt	State	1881

Name	Rank	Unit	Number
William Groves	Pvt	State	1744
John Green, 2nd	Pvt	State	413
Benjamin Gilbert	Pvt	State	1894
Thomas Gadd	Pvt	State	1614
Philip Graham	Pvt	Rec. 81	1720
Bennet George	Pvt	Rec. 81	1929
Lambert Goody	Pvt	Rec. 81	1721
John Gee	Pvt	Rec. 81	1767
Amos Griffith	Pvt	Rec. 81	3101
John Graham	Fifer	Rec. 81	2542
Charles Girdler	Pvt	State	883
		Rec. 81	2542
Thomas Gilham	Pvt	State	1710
Solomon Greene		Rec. 81	1477
Charles Goff	Pvt	1	884
John Gregory	Pvt	2	1605
James Gravey	Pvt	State	1545
William Greenage	Pvt	5	1296
Smart Greer	Pvt	Rec. 81	941
Samuel Gray	Pvt	State	1945
William George	Pvt	6	456
Southy George	Pvt	Rec. 81	943
Joseph Green	Pvt	State	1518
William Gudgeon	Pvt	Rec. 81	1494
John Gather	Pvt	5	1951
Jacob Games	Pvt	Rec 81	1739
Banjamin Gater	Pvt	Rec 81	1952
William Gillispie	Pvt	State	1599
Marshall Galloway	Pvt	3	1760
James Goodwin	Pvt	3	1784
William Grant	Pvt	Rec. 81	2019
Vincent/Wilson Gray	Pvt	Grayson's	1701
Michael Grosh	Pvt	German	1528
Robert Gelhampton	Pvt	4	1475
Thomas Grey	Pvt	4	78
Jacob Gray	Sgt	2	1870

Richard Gray	Pvt	2	915
John Giles	Pvt	2	401
Moses Graves	Pvt	5	1260
Jonathan Gill	M	Art	359
Mark Goldsborough		Art	289
Charles Groom	M	Art	416
Thomas Gleeson	M	Art	266
William Grimes	M	Art	1023
Enoch Ganet	Pvt	5	398
Harvey Gray	Pvt	7	1582
Sylvester Gatting	Pvt	1	3048
John Gordon	Pvt	Lee's Leg	165
Walter Glasgow	Pvt	3	1873
Wm. Hutton	Corp	Art	1021
Wm. Hellen	B	Art	3112
Cornelius Harling	M	Art	417
Michael Hughes	M	Art	1933
Wm. Hallen	B	Art	1933
(See Wm Hellen above)			[sic]
John Howard	M	Art	351
Jas. Hendrickson	M	Art	1420
Robert Harding	Pvt	1	151
Thos. Hart	Pvt	2	1478
Wm. Harper	Pvt	2	1190
John Hall	Pvt	2	217
Conrad Hodibuck	Pvt	2	1164
Joseph Hoole	Pvt	3	1016
John Hackett	Pvt	4	3116
Jeremiah Hooper	Pvt	4	1686
John Hulls	Pvt	4	1501
Isaac Hines	Pvt	4	1166
Josiah Hurley	Pvt	5	413
Richard Harper	Pvt	5	319
John Hall	Pvt	5	1209
Charles Heath	Pvt.	5	470
Ricard N. Haslip	Pvt	German	1488

Name	Rank	Unit	Number
Thomas Hutchcraft	Pvt	German	3888
Richard Hayes	Pvt	Rec. 81	4064
Wm. Hartman	Pvt	Rec. 81	277
James Humphries	Pvt	Rec. 81	1749
Hercules Hutchings	Pvt	Rec. 81	224
John Hannan	Pvt	Rec 81	322
Charles Hickey	Pvt	2	244
John Hutson, 2nd	Pvt	Rec. 81	1431
Calib Haley	Pvt	State	1925
John Holston	Pvt	Rec. 81	1976
Samuel Hughes	Pvt	Rec. 81	389
William Hamilton	D	3	321
Henry Harris	Pvt	3	245
Lawrence Hurdle	Pvt	7	225
Michael Hawke	Pvt	Art	1151
Henry Higgs	M	Art	276
Daniel Harvey	M	Art	361
John Head	M	Art	920
James Hutton	Sgt	Art	150
James Hammond	Corp	Art	4108
William Herrginton	Pvt	1	2559
Raphael Hagan	Pvt	1	93
John Head	Drummer	2	1378
John Hughes, 1st	Pvt	2	358
Richard Harper	Pvt	2	4032
James Hill	Pvt	2	2030
John Howard	Pvt	1	4061
John Holmes	Pvt	3	144
Richard Hurley	Pvt	3	3066
William Harris	Pvt	3	380
Elias Hardy	Pvt	3	95
Isaac Hill	Drummer	4	829
James Harris	Pvt	3	1383
John Howell	Pvt	4	267
William Howe	Pvt	4	218
Jacob Hines	Pvt	4	1451

Nathaniel Hull	Pvt	4	296
Henry Hines	Pvt.	3	1400
Zadock Harvey	Pvt	5	1326
Charles Hill	Pvt	6	310
Wm. Harris, 1st	Pvt	6	403
Nicholas Huster	Pvt	7	290
Thomas Hoye	Pvt	7	311
Walter Hagen	Pvt	7	1808
Randolph Hoskins	Pvt	1	1619
Lazarus Higgs	Pvt	State	222
James Hagan	Corp	State	3087
George Haden	Corp	5	926
Thomas Harris, 2nd	Sgt	Grayson's	2086
George Holton	Sgt	Rec. 81	1649
George Hagarthy	Sgt	2	1980
John Hood or Wood	Pvt	3	1718
Vachel Hays	Drummer	2	4065
James Hare	Pvt	2	1826
Samuel Hughes	Pvt	2	1320
Cornelius Howard	Sgt	3	1854
John B. Haslip	Pvt	3	31
Isaac Holliday	Pvt	4	1803
Leonard Hagan	Pvt	7	1338
Wm. Hughes	Pvt	1	496
John Higgens	Pvt	State	2081
John Hare	Pvt	State	3002
Peter Howard	Pvt	State	3011
John Hood, 2nd	Pvt	State	3029
John Hillary	Pvt	6	3006
John S. Hunt	Pvt	Rec. 81	102
Edward Hennisee	Pvt	1	1265
Pompey Hollis	Pvt	Rec. 81	154
James Halleron	Pvt	Rec. 81	1314
John Haynes	Pvt	Rec. 81	3075
David Hatton	Pvt	Rec.81	1216
Wm. Hamston		7	1430

Name	Rank	Company	Number
Samuel Harrison	Pvt	Rec. 81	1342
John Haney	Pvt	2	303
Austen Howard	Pvt	3	1136
Joseph Horsefield	Pvt	2	238
Joseph Hukell	Pvt	2	383
Barney Haney	Pvt	3	335
Richard Hall	Pvt	3	420
John Hamilton	Pvt	3	308
Peregrine Howard		3	362
Charles Harvey	Sgt	4	1743
John Hyde	Pvt	4	1642
Robert Harpham	Sgt	4	1915
Thomas Harris, 1st	Pvt	Rec. 81	4
Francis Hopkins	Pvt	3	3176
John Holder	Pvt	5	2557
John Harris, 1st	Pvt	5	1093
William Horney	Pvt	5	3115
John Hull	Drummer	5	1775
John Holliday	Pvt	6	1609
John Housley	Pvt	6	1906
John Hall, 2nd	Corp	6	1837
Jacob Hunt	Pvt	7	1836
Frederick Harty	Pvt	7	379
William Hurley	Pvt	7	1621
John Hulet	Pvt	7	400
John Harrell	Pvt	1	136
Joseph Hall	Pvt	1	36
John Haden	Pvt	7	1379
Wm. Hillman	Pvt	5	981
Walter Howe	Pvt	State	1395
Edward Holland	Drummer	State	3127
William Hick	Pvt	State	1517
George Hamilton	Pvt	State	134
Phillip Huston	Pvt	State	402
Nathan Harper	Pvt	State	1890
Samuel Hamilton	Pvt	State	481

Samuel Harper	Pvt	State	334
Lazarus Harmon	Pvt	State	11
Nehemiah Hadder	Pvt	State	4116
Ed. Hammond	Pvt	State	209
John Hancock	Pvt	State	249
Elijah Hutt	Pvt	State	1278
Ralph Hope	Pvt	Rev.81	190
Wm. Hill, 1st	Pvt	5	60
James Hewitt	Pvt	State	1419
James Harris, 2nd	Pvt	2	1521
Thomas Hawson	Pvt	1	1165
Stephen Hancock	Pvt	State	1243
John Hickens	Pvt	State	2037
Daniel Howe	Pvt	Rawlings	43
Richard Huggens	Sgt	Rawlings	332
Thomas Hill	Pvt	Rawlings	374
William Hope	Pvt	State	1976
John Hurley	Pvt	State	331
Leonard Holt	Pvt	State	1541
Nicholas Hiner	Pvt	4	1917
Richard Harrington	Pvt	Rec. 81	444
Levin Harrington	Pvt	Recruit 81	163
William Harper	Pvt	Recruit 81	3039
Daniel Holdman	Pvt	Recruit 81	169
John Hudson, 1st		Recruit 81	489
Samuel Hurst	Pvt	Recruit 81	1053
James Hudson, 1st	Pvt	2	299
William Hedge	Pvt	4	3887
William Hutcheson	Pvt	1	1806
William Harrison, 1st	Pvt	1	1702
Michael Hartman	Pvt	German	1045
John Hopkins	Pvt	7	1927
William Hammond	Pvt	7	1250
Henry Harley	Pvt	3	1323
James Homes		1	1317
Joseph Harper	Pvt	Rec 81	1289

Name	Rank	Unit	Number
John Harris, 2nd	Pvt	Rec 81	1241
Thomas Hammond	Pvt	Rec 81	1403
Daniel Hall	Pvt	7	1315
William Harris, 2nd	Pvt	6	4035
John Holliday, Sr.	Pvt.	6	495
James Hopkins		Hazen's	381
James Heaton		Hazen's	959
David Henderson		Lee's Leg	318
Joshua or Matthew Harvey		Lee's Leg	1463
Abijah Hickell		Lee's Leg	967
George Hill		Lee's Leg	181
Joseph Hemphill		Lee Leg	3095
Samuel Huggins		6	483
William Haney		Art	1325
William Hickenson	Pvt	Art	1394
Benton Harris	Pvt	State	58
Thomas Harrison, 1st	Pvt	2	344
Robert Johnston	Pvt	2	1829
Thomas Jones, 2nd	Pvt	5	1075
Zachariah Jacobs	Pvt	3	132
Thomas Jones, 3rd	Pvt	3	283
John Johnston, 3rd	Pvt		1872
Isaac Johnston	Pvt	Rawling's	486
William Johnston	Sgt	1	980
William Johnston	Sgt	German	824
Robert Issable	Sgt	2	1587
David Jones	Corp	2	269
John Johnston	Pvt	State	1864
William Joice, 2nd	Pvt		180
William Joice, 1st	Pvt	1	291
Archibald Johnston	Sgt	1	468
Edward Irvin	Pvt	1	255
Joseph Jenkins	Pvt	1	378
Henry Jacobs	Pvt	2	207
Nealy Jones	Pvt	2	279
Joseph Jones, 1st	Pvt	2	1179

Name	Rank	Unit	Number
William Jinkins	Pvt	2	1283
John Jones, 1st		2	2090
James Jackson	Sgt	2	1765
Benjamin Johnston	Fifer	3	1804
Thomas Jones, 1st	Pvt	3	895
Joseph Johnston	Pvt	4	4056
Adam Jameson	Pvt	4	161
John Johnston, 1st	Pvt	4	430
William Ingles	Pvt	5	1830
Aaron Jones	Pvt	5	46
Jesse Jacobs	Sgt	6	3074
Daniel Jarvis/Javins	Pvt	6	1586
Joseph Jeans	Sgt	Rawling's	827
Joseph Jones, Sr, 3rd	Pvt	State	2556
William Jones, 1st	Pvt	State	375
William Jones, 2nd	Pvt	State	1531
Jacob Jeffers	Pvt	Rec 81	1756
Thomas Johns	Pvt	Rec 81	889
Robert Johnston	Pvt	2	3175
John Jones, 2nd	Pvt	State	1270
Ed. Jackson	Pvt	Rec 81	86
Frederick Ijams	Pvt	Rec 81	1319
George Jennings	Pvt	State	1793
John Jackson	Pvt	State & 1	1285
Joseph Isaacs	Pvt	Rec 81	390
Abram Irvine	Pvt	2	76
Thomas Jones, 2nd	Pvt	Rec 80	1111
Charles Jones	Pvt	German	10
George Jones	Pvt	Rec 81	879
Thomas Jones, 4th	Pvt	Recruit 81	206
John Irons	Pvt	1	863
James Isaacs	Pvt	State	1371
Francis Johnston	M	Artillery	875
John Ireland	M	Artillery	1203
Philip Jones	M	Artillery	1099
Benedict Johnston	M	Artillery	231

John Jordan	Q.M.S.	5	3021
William Jones	Pvt	7	1156
John Jarvis		1	1321
Samuel Jenkins		Lee's Legion	4063
Thomas Johnston		Gist's	1914
Dennis Kelly	Sgt	1	1303
Edward Killman	Pvt	2	4154
James Kelly	Pvt	3	98
John King	Pvt	7	1516
Michael Kernon	Pvt	6	1967
William Kindle	Pvt	7	839
Walter Keech	Pvt		2004
Jacob Kiser	Pvt	German	107
John Knox, 1st	Pvt	4	1733
Joseph Carrick	Corp	6	1269
Francis Kitely	Pvt	7	179
Peter Kincade	Pvt	5	1754
Stephen Kemble	Pvt	3	230
William Kellow	Sgt	1	1312
Thomas King	Pvt	1	931
Adam Kephart	Pvt	2	1694
Jacob Knight	Pvt	2	4026
John Kidd	Pvt	4	1225
John King	Pvt	4	1229
William King	Pvt	4	1230
David Kelly	Pvt	5	1288
George Kelson	Pvt	5	1639
Benjamin H. Kerrick	Pvt	6	1157
James Kelly	Corp	7	1247
James Keckland	Pvt	7	1344
John Kildee	Pvt	State	112
Jacob Kelly	Pvt	Recruit 81	1248
Thomas P. Kittle	Pvt	Recruit 81	215
Benjamin Karns	Pvt	2	1887
Edward Kearsey	Pvt	6	77
James Knott	Pvt	State & 1	868

Name	Rank	Unit	No.
Edward Kirk	Pvt	Rawling's	918
Francis Kearns	Pvt	German	1313
David Kettle	Pvt	German	129
Abram Kettle	Pvt	German	1620
Matthew Kelly	Pvt	4	4095
John Knox, 2nd	Pvt	7	1257
James Killigan	Pvt	2	418
Nathaniel Knott	Pvt	3	1311
William Kennedy	Pvt	6	1695
Richard Kisby	Pvt	State	1191
David Kennedy		Hazen's	353
John Kennard		Lee's Legion	110
John Kincade		Lee's Legion	1276
Thomas Kearns		6	2500
George Laws	Pvt	2	1350
William Lettman	Pvt	2	280
William Lee	Pvt	2	1187
William Lilly	Pvt	3	410
John Loveday	Pvt	7	203
William Lucas	Pvt	1	288
Kinsey Lanham	Pvt	Recruit 81	309
John Lonass	Pvt	German	1015
Zachariah Lyles	Pvt	2	236
Thomas Lewis	Pvt	3	830
John Lowry	Pvt	7	4163
Darby Lanahan	Pvt	6	3133
Charles Leago	Pvt	German	1847
Jacob Lowe	Sgt	German	3067
Jonathan Lewis	Pvt	1	825
Michael Lloyd	Pvt	2	3037
William Laws	Pvt	2	1611
Roger Landers	Pvt	2	913
John Lucas, 1st	Pvt	2	1534
Benjamin Loffman	Pvt	5	1786
Levi Lord	Pvt	2	3005
Henry Laws	Pvt	3	3117

William Lynch	Pvt	3	1735
John Love, 1st		3	1233
John Lee, 1st	Pvt	3	1212
Michael Lawler	Pvt	3	1368
John Lynch, 2nd	Pvt	4	4030
Alexander Levi	Pvt	4	4024
Robert Legg	Pvt	State	202
John Linkon	Pvt	6	1984
Joseph Long	Pvt	6	1410
Joshua Leister	Pvt	7	4027
William Leakins	Pvt	7	1331
David Love	Sgt	7	1994
Francis Long	Pvt	State	3038
John Lewin	Pvt	State	1409
Christopher Lambert	Pvt	State	99
George Linton	Pvt	State	1263
Paul Lapine	Pvt	State & 1	433
Dudley Lee	Pvt	6	301
Theophilus Lindsay	Pvt	1	1120
Thomas Larrimore	Pvt	German	1811
Joseph Lewis, 2nd	Pvt	Recruit 81	1273
John Lynch, 3rd	Pvt	Rawlings	3028
John Lesley	Pvt	Recruit 81	826
William Lee, 2nd	Pvt	Recruit 81	284
Thomas Long	Pvt	3	1237
Nehemiah Lingard	Pvt	Recruit 81	3022
Timothy Langrell	Pvt	Recruit 81	1226
Jesse Locker	Pvt	Recruit 81	1493
William Little	Pvt	3	4040
Theophilus Lomax	Sgt	5	373
Edward Legg	Pvt	State	1613
Thomas Loveday (Lovely)	D	Rawling's	1447
Dennis Leary	Pvt	State	1374
Robert Livingston	M	Artillery	990
Joshua Lovely	M.	Artillery	1791
Richard Lewis	Sgt	Artillery	1526

Name	Rank	Unit	Number
Peter Laurence	M	Artillery	1316
Jacob Lion	Sgt	Artillery	254
Daniel Longest	Pvt	3	3111
John Lavender	Pvt	3	1017
James Lowry	Pvt	5	916
John Laton	Pvt	5	1741
John Lindsay	Pvt	4	187
Barney Lemmon	Pvt	4	350
Peter Leddington	Pvt	1	3026
Jeremiah Lee	Pvt	5	171
Thomas or John Luff	Pvt	3	802
John Majors	Pvt	1	247
Richard Mudd	Sgt	1	1687
Walter Miles	Corp	1	1448
Gifford Minikee	Pvt	1	1234
William Mann	Pvt	2	3049
James Magraw	Pvt	2	370
Frederick Miles	Corp	2	1853
John Morris	Corp	3	1012
Valentine Murray	Corp	3	404
Jonathan Mayhew	Corp	3	1346
John Miles, 1st	Corp	3	1048
James Matthews	Corp	4	1183
William Marshal	Corp	5	3141
Robert Matthews	Corp	6	256
Thomas McCernan	Corp	5	352
John Mantle	Sgt	6	377
John Mattingly	Pvt	7	1363
Arthur McClain	Sgt	7	469
Samuel McConnell	Sgt	6	208
Joseph McNamara	Pvt	State	2039
Jeremiah Mudd	Sgt	State	327
John Matthews, 2nd	Sgt	State	1000
John Moore, 3rd	Sgt	State	286
Hezikiah Massey	Sgt	5	1415
John McCay, 1st	Sgt	State	871

John McDonald	Fifer	Recruit 81	1334
Michael Maguire	Pvt	3	1324
Thomas Mahoney	Pvt	German	242
Stephen Magraw	Pvt	German	339
Jacob Moses, 2nd	Pvt	German	1699
Bennet Mudd	Sgt	1	1297
Humphrey Miniken	Pvt	4	4099
Benjamin McHaffee	Pvt	5	94
Benjamin Moran	Pvt	6	3043
John Martin, 2nd	Pvt	6	1559
Christian Myers	Pvt	7	1050
John M. Laughlin	Pvt	7	320
Andrew Moore	Pvt	7	1277
William Martin	Corp	6	845
Timothy McLamar	Pvt	State	1010
Michael McGower	Pvt	State	3179
Joseph McAtee	Pvt	State	252
Thomas Mahoney	Pvt	6	221
Thomas Maloney	Pvt	7	3050
Michael Miller	Pvt	1	59
Darby McNamara	Pvt	1	4102
John Martindale	Fife Maj	1	1286
Peter McNaughton	Sgt	1	1722
John Morrison	Fifer	1	1622
Wm. McLaughlin	Pvt	2	1486
Christopher McGraw	Drummer	2	1125
James Mason	Pvt	2	4106
Wm. Moore, 1st	Pvt	2	1778
Richard Mitchel	Pvt	2	3070
Wn. Moore, 2nd	Pvt	2	205
John Martin, 1st		2	1372
Cornelius McLaughlin	Pvt	3	1056
Charles Murphy	Sgt	3	3157
Wm. McGee	Pvt	3	1389
John Matthews, 1st	Pvt	3	1388
Charles McGee	Pvt	3	355

Matthew Moore, 1st	Pvt	3	235
Wm. Mitchell	Pvt	3	1390
John McCann	Pvt	3	1079
Patrick Mahorn	Pvt	3	1404
Matthew Moore, 2nd	Pvt	4	1843
Thomas Murphy	Pvt	4	387
Christopher McAway	Pvt	4	1965
Hugh McMillan	Sgt	4	1856
James Mead	Drum Maj		2429
John McCoy	Pvt	5	1364
George Mantle	Pvt	6	939
Michael McCann	Pvt	6	336
James Maxwell	Corp	6	285
William Moore, 3rd	Pvt	6	106
Boston Medler	Drummer	7	2012
Wm. Mann, 1st	Pvt	7	384
John Moore, 1st	Pvt	7	425
Charles McNable	Sgt	7	1220
Joseph Managa	Pvt	7	4060
Joseph Murphey	Pvt	7	1724
Peter Maguire	Pvt	7	1098
John Mccannally	Pvt	7	3013
Enoch McClain	Sgt	7	3108
John Maxwell, 1st	Pvt	7	3153
William Moade	Pvt	7	4043
John Mick	Pvt	7	294
Neal Morris	Pvt	7	999
John Mills, 2nd	Pvt	6	1979
Nicholas Milburn	Pvt	6	5
William McNeal	Corp	6	274
James McDonald	Pvt	7	4037
Thos. Matthews	Corp	State	1629
John McGuinis	Pvt	State	1287
Isachea Mason	Corp		813
William Manly	Pvt	State	1962
Henry Mansfield	Pvt	State	2540

Name	Rank	Unit	Number
John Moore, 2nd	Pvt	State	966
John C. Miller	Pvt	State	482
Jesse McKinsey	Pvt	German	234
John McNeill	Pvt	4	419
John Moore, 4th	Pvt	4	307
Adam Mushler*	Pvt	German	251
John McGall	Pvt	Recruit 81	1706
David Meadows	Pvt	Recruit 81	1280
Roderick McKinsey	Pvt.	Rawlings	87
Aaron Michell	Pvt	Recruit 81	1640
Aleard Melville	Pvt	Recruit 81	1966
Robt Mitchell		Recruit 81	1509
Daniel Murphy	Pvt	Recruit 81	211
Francis McCann	Pvt	Recruit 81	1548
John Morris, 2nd	Pvt	Recruit 81	1393
John Mills, 3rd	Pvt	7	3170
John Murray, 1st	Pvt	7	1719
John McDonald	Sgt		141
John McKnight	Fifer		135
Edward Mahoney	Pvt	State	330
Benjamin Marsh	Pvt	1	968
Wm. Marlow	Sgt	Rawling's	1612
Luke Merriam	Pvt	Recruit 81	910
John McCaliff	Drummer	Recruit 81	1795
Wm. Mansfield	Pvt	State	1215
John Maglin	Pvt	State	4033
Daniel Mann	Pvt	State	1709
Peter Melvin	Pvt	2	1801
John McClain	Pvt	3	1367
John Moore, 5th	Pvt	7	983
Thomas Matthews, 2nd	Pvt	Recruit 81	2026
Joshua McKinsey	Pvt	German	882
Moses McKinsey	Pvt	German	3020
Francis McGauran	Sgt	German	1939

*Prob. George Adam Mohler

Name	Rank	Unit	Number
Patrick McKinsey	Pvt	Rawlings	1088
John McBride	Pvt	Rawlings	326
Thos. McKinsey	Pvt	Rawlings	323
Zachariah Mills	Pvt	Recruit 81	3114
Abraham Manning	Pvt	Recruit 81	1238
Thomas Mie	Pvt	2	1396
John Milstead	Pvt	1	140
James Moore	G	Artillery	1356
Peter Maynor	Fifer	Artillery	108
Charles Muiritt	M	Artillery	1397
Robert Myers	M	Artillery	395
Dennis McCormick	Corp	Artillery	1349
Phillip Masterson	M	Artillery	860
Hugh McDowell	M	Artillery	492
Peter Maynor, Sr	M	Artillery	363
John McGowen	M	Artillery	1535
Cruise Moser	Pvt	2	396
James Murphy	Pvt	2	4064
John McDougle	Pvt	2	3034
John McConnikin	Pvt	2	1261
John McGran	Pvt	2	1547
John Murray (Bugley's Co)	Pvt	3	1290
John Miller	Pvt	2	24
Richard Maxwell	Pvt	4	1711
Archibald Morton	Pvt	4	369
John McIntosh	Pvt	5	3092
Thomas Morgan	Pvt	5	1100
Dennis Murley	Pvt	5	1557
Wm. McKinley	Pvt	6	1646
Barney McManus	Pvt	7	1944
Jacob Moses	Pvt	3	3104
William Matthews	Pvt	6	4062
Jacob Myers	Pvt	State & 2	325
Timothy McMahon	Pvt	3	1106
Patrick Mollohon	Pvt	Recruit 81	1930
Wm. McPherson	Pvt	Recruit 81	3077

George Miller	Pvt	Recruit 81	1779
Nicholas McManiard	Pvt	Recruit 81	1029
James McIntire	Pvt	Hazen's	1989
John McColgan	Pvt	Hazen's	50
Charles March or Marsh	Pvt	Hazen's	2532
Alex. Matthewson	Pvt	Hazen's	155
George McDonald	Pvt	Hazen's	977
Martin Malloy	Pvt	Hazen's	847
Jamer McCrakin	Pvt	Lee's Legion	49
John Manley	Pvt	Lee's Legion	1240
Hugh McCoy	Pvt	1	372
Marmaduke McDonald	Pvt	3	1822
James McCarty	Pvt	4	1113
Nicholas Nicholson	Sgt	1	1519
John Neary	Sgt	1	1081
Asael Nicholls	Pvt	3	1129
John Neighbors	Pvt	7	137
John Newton, 2nd	Pvt	State	3160
Michael Noland	Pvt	6	1896
Richard Nelson	Pvt	State	1173
Patrick Nolan	Pvt	State	1947
Thomas Neill	Pvt	1	1259
Henry Nicholson	Corp	2	1332
Stephen Nicholson	Sgt	2	1348
Wm. Newton	Pvt	2	1630
Morris Neagell	Pvt	3	1514
Wm. A. Needhand	Sgt	4	1274
Joseph Nabb	Pvt	5	1987
Wm. Nailor	Pvt	5	450
James Narvel	Fifer	6	4028
Isaac Nicholls	Pvt	Recruit 81	113
Basil Norman	Pvt	7	1281
Wm. Niblet	Pvt	7	1564
John Newton, 1st	Pvt	Recruit 81	894
Charles Nabb	Pvt	7	177
John Nelson	Pvt	4	6

Name	Rank	Unit	Number
John Nevit, 2nd	Pvt	2	152
Joseph Neale	Pvt	Rawlings	367
John Nicholson	Pvt	Recruit 81	3041
John Nave	Pvt	Recruit 81	111
James Neale	M	Artillery	186
Daniel Neal	M	Artillery	253
Martin Noble		2	1384
Nathaniel Nott			127
George Nicholson		4	2543
Samuel J. Nelme		Artillery	1869
Leonard Outerbridge	Pvt	2	1358
Samuel Oram	Pvt	4	1009
John Obrian	Pvt	State	2038
John Osborn	Pvt	3	3007
Joseph Overereck	Pvt	3	3025
Daniel O'Quinn	Pvt	4	1031
Stephen Owens	Pvt	6	1723
James Owens	Pvt	5	2522
Charles Orme	Pvt	7	1040
Henry Osten or Austin	Pvt	2	955
John Onion	Fifer	State	3155
Peter Outhouse	Pvt	State	1495
Samuel Owens	Pvt	1	1202
Michael Obrian	B	Artillery	37
Philip Obrian	Corp	Artillery	219
Michael O'Farrel	M	Artillery	869
Jacob Owens	M	Artillery	4034
John Owens	Pvt	3	1538
Richard O'Quynn	Pvt	German	1968
Elijah Oakley	Pvt	Recruit 81	1855
Joseph Owens	Pvt	Lee's Legion	985
James Onants	Pvt		842
James Parker	Pvt	Rawlings	2426
Nathan Peak	Sgt	1	834
Henry Phillips	Pvt	2	1889
Cupid Plummer	Pvt	2	1792

Name	Rank	Regiment	Number
George Pattrick	Pvt	Rawling's	995
Gabriel Peters	Pvt	5	1279
John Purdy	Pvt	6	405
Henry Purdy	Pvt	6	1991
George Phillips	Pvt	7	1644
John Pease	Sgt	7	1114
Jesse Powers	Pvt	State	1110
Obadiah Plummer	Pvt	2	3042
Thomas Phipps	Pvt	2	809
Samuel Pleasants	Pvt	4	248
James Phillips	Pvt	State	488
George Plumley	Pvt	State	3017
Thomas Pollhouse	Pvt	German	3110
Thomas Peacock	Pvt	7	1895
John Pickering	Pvt	2	3000
William Poland	Pvt	1	2008
Simon Perry	Pvt	1	1327
William Pherson		1	1264
Aquilla Pearce	D	2	1128
William Purchase	Corp	2	198
John Peany	D	2	1137
Stephen Preston	Pvt	3	287
Richard Proctor	Pvt	3	424
William Peters	Pvt	3	1251
William Pursell	Pvt	4	388
William Prior	Pvt	4	3100
William Pecker	Pvt	4	3163
Joseph Purdy	D. Maj	5	1047
James Poole	Pvt	5	2041
George Pierce	Pvt	5	1598
Neal Peacock	Pvt	7	1798
Stephen Price	Sgt	6	1600
Elijah Pepper	Pvt	7	1645
Thomas Pinder	Pvt	State	2567
Thomas Pennyfield	Pvt	State	862
Lambert Phillips	Pvt	State	1990

Thomas Patterson	Pvt	Recruit 81	160
Nathaniel Price	Pvt	Recruit 81	1583
Thomas Perry	Pvt	Recruit 81	1546
Joshua Pierce	Pvt	1	837
Michael Pilkerton		5	3014
Joseph Pherson	Corp	1	1399
William Prather	Fifer	Recruit 81	478
William Paul	Pvt	Recruit 81	104
Thomas Porter	Pvt	Recruit 81	1476
Robert Pennington	Pvt	5	836
William Porter	Pvt	Recruit 81	4047
William Pagram	Pvt	2	2546
Thomas Pettit		Recruit 81	1357
Arthur Pritchet	Pvt	Recruit 81	4054
Joseph Pogue	M.	Artillery	329
Thomas Potter	Fifer	ARtillery	1097
John Prout	M	Artillery	2534
John Paine	M	Artillery	422
Francis Popha,	M	Artillery	487
John Pearsonm	M	Artillery	2089
Jonas Phillips	M	Artillery	1429
Benjamin Phelps	Pvt	2	81
Joseph Peters		2	72
James Pritchard		2	1365
Andrew Preston		2	1975
Emanuel Polston		4	175
James Paivel		5	1352
James Pack		6	473
Thomas Price		6	1201
Jacob Plaine		Lee's Legion	237
John Parkinson	Pvt	1	3169
John Parsons	Pvt	6	1103
Edward Purdy		6	1555
John Quick	Sgt	2	3177
John Quinn	Pvt	3	1336
William Quinton	Pvt	7	948

Patrick Quinn	Pvt	Rawlings	1437
John Quinn	M	Artillery	1500
James Quay	Pvt	1	1246
William Rowles	Pvt	4	1441
William Roberts, 1st	Pvt	1	125
Andrew Riggs	Pvt	2	1946
Edward Richardson	Pvt	3	801
John Rock	Pvt	3	1943
William Rock	Pvt	3	4164
Jeremiah Rodes	Pvt	3	1355
Adam Raines	Pvt	3	1707
John Robertson	Pvt	3	306
Robert Richardson	Pvt	3	1443
Thomas Redman	Pvt	4	304
Benedict Reynolds	Pvt	3 or 4	1213
Bennet Rawlings	Pvt	3	1005
Robert Rise	Pvt	6	956
Michael Rhytmire	Pvt	German	823
Edward Riely	Pvt	State	1770
Alexander Rutherford	Pvt	State	3018
William Richardson	Pvt	State	3040
John Radley	Sgt	4	88
James Ryly	Pvt	3	910
Charles Reynolds	Sgt	State	354
Charles Riddle	Pvt	Recruit 81	833
Horatio Roberts	Pvt	7	4055
William Rogers	Pvt	1	831
Cristian Ross	Pvt	Recruit 81	1158
William Smith	Pvt	1	961
Thomas Sanders	Pvt	1	1787
William Smith	Pvt	1	1492
John Snelling	Pvt	1	1746
Anthony Smith	D	1	1772
David Smith	Pvt	2	870
Leonard Swan	Pvt	3	1335
Jesse Simons	Corp	3	3030

Thomas Smith	Pvt	4	1648
Andrew Stewart	Pvt	2	1700
Thomas Sappington	Sgt	5	1769
William Sharp	Corp	5	1998
William Simmons	Pvt	Recruit 80	1684
John Stackhouse	Pvt	6	3019
Michael Sours	Pvt	6	1751
Aquilla Smith	Pvt	7	2023
William Sly	Corp	7	3132
Jeremiah Sullivan	Pvt	State	1385
Richard Smith	Sgt	State	1345
Alexander or Andrew Smith	Pvt	5	1018
Samuel Scott	Pvt	State	157
Benjamin Smith	Pvt	Recruit 80	3016
James Stewart, 1st	Pvt	Recruit 80	1532
John Smith	Pvt	3	2022
Leonard Smith	Pvt	State	908
Nathan Speak	Pvt	6	1242
Frederick Stoffee	Pvt	Recruit 81	196
Edward Sute	Corp	2	453
Murphy Shee	Pvt	Recruit 81	1359
George Silver	Pvt	German	1046
Joseph Smith	Pvt	3	142
John Smithard	Pvt	German	2032
Robert Shipley	Pvt	2	1239
William Sherley	Pvt	State	117
Ignatius	Pvt	Recruit 81	900
Jonathan Short	Sgt	Recruit 81	214
Josiah Smith	Sgt	State	897
Charles Schoudrick	Corp	5	1398
Robert Scriviner	Sgt	2	3134
Thomas Stokes	Pvt	2	360
Noah Sears	Pvt	3	1301
James Stewart, 2nd	Pvt	4	1337
Rueben Smith	Pvt	4	184
Abraham Shockee	Pvt	Gist's	1002

Name	Rank		No.
Peter Smith	Sgt	1	1217
Wm. Sykes	Pvt	1	227
Charles Scott	Pvt	1	1143
John Smith, 2nd	Pvt	7	1306
Humphrey Spencer	Sgt	2	1293
Jesse Suite	Sgt	2	859
John Salmon	Pvt	2	2536
James Shaur	Pvt	2	1512
John Shouell	Pvt	2	1977
Aaron Spalding	Sgt	2	1438
James Smith, 2nd	Pvt	3	1036
John Smith, 4th	Corp	2	2003
John Scott	Drummer	3	937
William Smith, 2nd	D	4	371
Conrad Smith	Pvt	4	1299
Thos. Slade	Pvt	4	44
Elijah Smith	Pvt	4	2017
Wm. Sinclair	Pvt	5	1073
Levy Smith	Sgt	5	1391
Daniel Smith, 1st	Pvt	5	1868
Wm. Sullivan	Pvt	5	1807
John Smith, 1st	Corp	5	1078
Perry Sullivan	Pvt	5	2083
Roger Shorter	Pvt	5	832
Solomon Summers	Pvt	5	124
George Sanders	Pvt	5	1401
Robert Sharpless	Corp	6	1200
Alexander Stephenson	Drummer	6	40
John Summers	Pvt	6	1206
Wm. Stonestreet	Pvt	6	1347
Joseph Sloop	Pvt	6	1445
James Sewall	Pvt	6	3109
Thomas Smith, 1st	Pvt	6	1030
Michael Standly	Pvt	6	3889
George Steem or Stumm	Pvt	6	1370
James Smith, 3rd	Pvt	7	1726

Christopher Simpkins	Pvt ... 7	28
Abraham Stallins	Drummer 7	178
Peter Stephens	Pvt ... 7	890
Daniel Smith, 2nd	Pvt ... 7	2502
Christopher Seymore	Pvt ... State	1902
James Sullivan	Pvt ... State	282
John Smith, 3rd	Pvt ... State	1782
John Shanks	Pvt ... State	1223
Bennet Sherley, 2nd	Pvt ... State	1025
Job Sylvester	Pvt ... State	143
Levi Scott	Drummer State	1783
Robert Streets	Pvt ... State	1484
Wm. Sterling	Pvt ... State	39
John Smallwood, 2nd	Pvt ... State	1435
John Smallwood, 1st	Pvt ... Recruit 81	1054
John Starkey	Pvt ... Recruit 81	1186
James Shepherd	Pvt ... Recruit 81	2028
John Spire	Pvt ... Recruit 81	1777
Chas. Sickle	Pvt ... Recruit 81	1937
Solomon Sullivan	Pvt ... Recruit 81	73
Richard Spires	Pvt ... Recruit 81	1198
John Sheffer	Pvt ... Recruit 81	1862
Salday Stanley	Pvt ... Recruit 81	368
Thomas Smith, 2nd	Pvt ... State	1544
Luke Sanson	Pvt ... 7	228
Thomas Summers	Pvt ... 2	4112
William Silwood	Pvt ... German	1857
Benjamin Steward	Pvt ... State	1124
Laurence Simpson	Pvt ... Recruit 81	61
William Steward	Fifer or Pvt	61440
John Stoffle or Stoffe	... Recruit 81	1731
Philip Savoy	Pvt ... 1	1479
Samuel Street	Fifer .. 4	173
Joseph Sidney or Sidmer	Pvt ... 5	2031
Elias Smith	Pvt ... 6	1308
Michael Smith, 2nd	Pvt ... German	954

Christopher/Christian Smith	Pvt	German	3041
Eichael Smith, 1st	Pvt	German	927
Samuel F. Shoemaker	Pvt	German	1001
John Stanton	Pvt	German	922
Oliver Stephens	Pvt	Recruit 81	1096
Cato Snowden	Pvt	Recruit 81	1153
Basil Shaw	Sgt	Rawling's	2080
Thos. Scoudrick	Pvt	5	3149
Joseph Southall	Pvt	3	1091
Thomas Sheridan	Pvt	1 - 81	1732
Walter B. Smallwood	Pvt	Recruit 81	1180
William Standley	Pvt	State	934
James Sappington	Pvt	Recruit 81	1961
James Smith, 1st	Pvt	German	1439
Jacob Standley	Pvt	7	1375
James Scott	Sgt	State	3158
George Scone	Corp	5	45
William Sizeland	Pvt	7	411
Joseph H. Spencer	Sgt	2	1810
Henry Slack	Sgt	Artillery	491
John Slack	Sgt	Artillery	1926
Charles Sutton	Sgt	Artillery	1145
John Sillman	M	Artillery	1341
William Stalker	M	Artillery	1055
Robert Smith	M	Artillery	2538
Rueben Scott	M	Artillery	1955
Thomas Smith	M	Artillery	1533
James Simmonds	M	Artillery	442
Andrew Shrink	M	Artillery	3046
John Sandall	M	Artillery	1133
John Standley, Jr	M	Artillery	2560
John Smith	M	Artillery	892
Thomas Standley	M	Artillery	929
Rawling Spinks	M	Artillery	1219
Valentine Smith	Pvt	1	3036
Thomas Salsbury	Pvt	1	1865

Name	Rank		No.
Nathaniel Smith	Pvt	1	1745
Richard Sweeny	Pvt	2	1821
John Smith	Sgt	2	2013
James Sweeny	Pvt	2	451
Thomas Sergeant	Pvt	2	2533
Charles Snow	Pvt	2	3173
Charles Simpson	Pvt	2	1590
John Sanders		3	1008
James Sheridan	Pvt	3	2007
Joseph Spinks	Pvt	3	4053
Jeremiah Scrabbles	Pvt	3	1014
John Spriggs	Pvt	3	423
James Simms	Sgt	3	952
Thomas Sylvester	Pvt	5	1174
Darby Sullivan	Pvt	5	1376
Robert Sturton	Pvt	5	216
Noble Simmons		6	293
William Spyers		6	409
John Sloop		6	1462
John Shaw		7	1823
Patrick Scott	Pvt	7	440
Peter Shoemaker		7	452
John Sankey		7	2398
William Smith			944
William Smith		Hazen's	1815
Barthelolomew Sheridan		Hazen's	984
George Summerville		Hazen's	3052
John Strahan		Lee's Legion	1912
Abraham Sutton		Lee's Legion	1654
Tamerlane Spencer		Artillery	1405
Phillip Shoebrick	Invalid	2	1362
Edward Timms	Pvt	1	281
John Tucker	Pvt	1	2530
Dennis Tramwell	Pvt	1	878
William Townsend	Pvt	7	1584
Richard Taylor	Pvt	7	1773

Francis Thompson	Pvt	1	1084
Solomon Turner	Pvt	7	1908
Giles Thompson or Thomas	Pvt	State	1747
Samuel Trigg	Pvt	3	250
John Tomlin	Pvt	German	464
Peter Tippet	Pvt	3	70
John Trusty	Pvt	3	1496
Samuel Taylor	Pvt	7	1116
Thomas Tanner	Pvt	7	1161
James Tite	Pvt	German	4101
Anthony Tucker	Pvt	5	1759
Christopher Touchstone	Pvt	6	1069
William Taylor	Pvt	1	996
Natley Tippet	Pvt	1	392
William Toland	Pvt	2	1305
Lambert Thompsen	Pvt	2	1377
John Taylor, 1st	Pvt	2	1960
James Thomas, Jr	Pvt	3	3103
John Turner, 3rd	Pvt	3	3068
Bartholomew Tompson	Pvt	2	1696
Richard Tasco	Pvt	3	1513
Henry Townley	Pvt	3	333
Thomas Thompson	Pvt	3	118
Peter Topping	Pvt	4	1708
John Taylor, 2nd	Pvt	4	1193
Evin Tumbleson	Pvt	4	4025
Robert Taylor, 2nd	Sgt	5	903
Cornelius Tomson	Pvt	5	3003
George Taylor	Pvt	5	1690
John Turner	Pvt	7	2036
James Terry	Pvt	3	3124
William Taylor, 2nd	Pvt	Rawling's	1969
William Taylor Jr, 3rd	Pvt	7	2529
James Thomas Sr	Sgt	State	1064
Allen Towsend	Pvt	Recruit 81	1392
Levin Thomas	Pvt	Recruit 81	3012

Name	Rank	Unit	Number
James Tigner	Pvt	Recruit 81	2503
John Tomson, 1st	Pvt	Recruit 81	975
Edward Tanner	Pvt	Recruit 81	1529
Thomas Thomas	Pvt	Recruit 81	199
John D. Tully	Pvt	Recruit 81	942
John Thomas, 2nd	Pvt	Recruit 81	232
George Twench	Sgt	Rawling's	394
Henry Tucker, 2nd	Sgt	Recruit 81	820
John Turner, 2nd	Sgt	7	1796
John Thomas, 1st	Sgt	6	74
Samuel Tindall	Sgt	3	957
Joseph Thompson	Sgt	3	865
Thomas Tyack	Sgt	Artillery	1087
John Turner	M	Artillery	1195
Rezin Thacknill	Pvt	1	1485
James Trego	Pvt	2	126
William Tutten	Pvt	2	1999
John Tuff	Pvt	6	1387
John Thomas	Pvt	6	4098
Aaron Townsend	Pvt	7	807
John Turner (of Morris' Co)	Pvt	7	109
Francis Taylor	Pvt	Recruit 81	122
Evan Thomas	Pvt	Recruit 81	1222
Dennis Ternan	Pvt	7	1406
Francis Tycowit	Pvt	Hazen's	64
John Towlin		Lee's Legion	1502
John German Thomas		Lee's Legion	1386
Jesse Thompson	Sgt	Artillery	856
Cornelius Vaughan	Pvt	German	1942
Stephen Varlow	Pvt	2	3071
John Varlow	Pvt	5	1523
Edward Vickers	Pvt	State	1080
William Vaughan	Pvt	2	1192
John Vincent	Pvt	2	917
John Vanzant	Pvt	4	1122
Samuel Vermillion	Pvt	1	1886

Name	Rank	Unit	Number
George Vernon	Pvt	State	1171
John Vaughan	Sgt	Artillery	1071
James Veazy		Lee's Legion	3047
Thomas Woolford	Pvt	German	1834
Daniel Williams	Pvt	German	275
John Williams	Pvt	1	1450
George Ward, 1st	Pvt	1	431
David Williams	Pvt	2	243
William Wheatley	Pvt	2	223
Andrew Wingate	Pvt	2	366
York Waters	Pvt	2	1809
Samuel B. White	Pvt	3	2009
George Winham	Pvt	3	145
William West	Pvt	3	1254
William Wilkeson	Pvt	3	1623
Charles Williams, 1st	Pvt	3	1641
George Willson	Pvt	5	3045
Jonathan Windell	Pvt	6	139
Michael Wiser	Pvt	7	4048
Motley Whitcomb	Pvt	7	1774
Gabriel Williams	Sgt	7	1414
Richard Wheeler	Corp	State	1413
James Whitcomb	Pvt	State	919
Walter Watson	Pvt	State	71
Benjamin Ward	Sgt	State	1601
Joseph White	Pvt	5	904
Sylvester Wheatley	Pvt	2	1466
Jonathan Weeden	Pvt	Rawling's	1007
Alexander West	Pvt	1	1184
William Willson	Pvt	7	1353
Edward Wright	Pvt	4	1262
William Wedge	Pvt	7	982
John Willing	Pvt	Recruit 81	2425
Phillip Welsh	Pvt	Rec. 81 & 4	2548
John Wilkerson	Pvt	Recruit 81	119
Samuel Wright	Pvt	German	1988

Name	Rank	Unit	Number
George Watson	Pvt	State	1322
Charles Willett	Pvt	Recruit 81	1552
John Willing	formerly Artillery		998
John Wade, 1st	Pvt	German	35
Edward Wade, 2nd	Pvt	3	1101
William Whaland	Pvt	Recruit 81	978
John Willis	Pvt	Recruit 81	1900
Nicholas Welch	Pvt	Recruit 80	315
Benjamin Williams, 3rd	Pvt	Recruit 81	1897
Thomas Wood, 3rd	Pvt	Recruit 81	877
Thomas Windom	Sgt	1	3106
John T. West	Fifer	1	3069
Jonathan White	Pvt	1	886
Jesse Wright	Pvt	2	1412
John Welch, 1st	Pvt	2	885
Thomas Wood, 1st	Pvt	2	1558
James Willson, 1st	Pvt	2	1986
Thomas Wimber	Pvt	2	2087
Thomas Wate or Wyatt	Pvt	2	343
Robert Walker	Pvt	3	302
Michael Woolford	Pvt	3	1560
Frederick Wilmott	Pvt	3	3122
Thomas Watson	Pvt	3	408
John Williams, 1st	Pvt	3	2558
Barney Wilson	Pvt	3	912
Robertson Wood	Pvt	4	1268
Thomas Wood, 2nd	Pvt	4	1380
Jeremiah Williams	Corp	4	1776
James Wood, 2nd	Pvt	4	1606
Daniel Willis	D	5	1936
David Willson	Pvt	5	1842
John Wilkenson	Sgt	5	1764
Daniel Warrior	D	6	1713
Michael Wiery	Fifer	6	1468
Benjamin Williams, 2nd	Pvt	6	2523
Absolum Wright	Pvt	6	835

William Willson, 2nd	Pvt	Rawling's	2554
Samuel Wedge	Pvt	7	92
James White	Pvt	7	1361
Michael Waltman	Pvt	7	3089
John Wells	Pvt	State	3150
Richard Weily	Pvt	State	1453
John Willson, 1st	Pvt	State	51
Rhody Woodland	Pvt	State	1938
John Walker, 3rd	Sgt	State, late 1	1470
Banks Webb	Pvt	State	1899
John West, 2nd	Pvt	State	2020
William Watkins	Drummer	State	2006
James Willson, 2nd	Pvt	State	1647
Charles Wheeler	Pvt	Recruit 81	4050
George Williams	Sgt	Recruit 81	1024
Humphrey Wells	Pvt	Recruit 81	1594
Wm. Willson, 1st	Pvt	Recruit 81	958
James West	Pvt	Recruit 81	3096
James Wood, 1st	Sgt	Recruit 81	1034
John Wright	Pvt	Recruit 81	3076
Zadock Whaley	Pvt	7	1766
Anthony Weaver	Pvt	1	2041
Benjamin Williams, 1st	Pvt	7	185
Wm. Whitton or Whittaker	Pvt	Recruit 81	1366
John Walker, 1st	Pvt	German	2550
John Welch, 2nd	Pvt	2	1596
James Williams	Pvt	Recruit 81	861
Samuel Willson	Sgt	State	3128
Edward Walter	Pvt	Recruit 81	974
Jarvis Williams	Pvt	4	4058
James Welch	B	Artillery	2082
James Whaling	G	Artillery	4067
James Welch	M	Artillery	1618
Thomas Williams	Drummer	Artillery	4057
Wm. Withorm or Whitton	M	Artillery	83
David White	M	Artillery	1039

David Welch	Sgt	Artillery	1817
John Wheeler		Artillery	1734
Thomas Webster		2	880
Wm. Willson		2	1597
James Welch		2	1140
Peter Ward		2	1844
Zachariah Williams		3	1616
James Williams		5	1615
Abraham Warters		5	1892
Solomon Watts		5	1944
David Woods		6	2021
John Waters		6	4023
Thos. Wheeler		7	204
Garret Welch		Recruit 81	1422
Benjamin Willson		Hazen's	964
Edward White		Hazen's	1655
Edward Wall		Hazen's	970
John Wysham		Lee's Legion	89
John Ward		Lee's Legion	2015
William Wade	M	Artillery	1469
Samuel Young	Pvt	6	1449
John Young, 2nd	Corp	6	2552
Godfrey Young	Pvt	6	1715
Jacob Yeast or Yost	Pvt	Recruit 81	1188
Henry Young	Pvt	Recruit 81	3024
John Young, 1st	Pvt	4	1090
David Young	M	Artillery	1013
Richard Yates		2	991
William York		7	1819
Jacob Young	Drummer	Recruit 81	3073
Thomas Yeates		Artillery	2091

PATENTS

Auxiliary. Re-surveyed for George Calmes, the 18th day of May 1827, and patented to Lucy Perry, 17th day of March 1841. Lots: 892, 905, 906, 907, 922, 974, 975, 978, 979.

Anderson's Settlement. Re-surveyed for Nathan A. Lower, the -- day of --, 1849; unpatented. Lots: 909, 918, as vacancy Nos.

Addition to White Plains. 305 acres. Re-surveyed for David Lynn, 22 June 1830, and patented to David Lynn April 15, 1831. Lots: 958, 960, 963, 1008, 1012, 1013.

Avondale. Re-surveyed for Thomas Perry, 26 June 1850, and patented 7 June 1851. Lots: 1110, 1111, 1112, 1716, 1717, 1718, 1623.

Arden Corrected, 1150 acres. Re-surveyed for Charles Nourse and George Templeman, 1 December 1841, and patented to them 16 January 1843. Lots: 3206, 3207, 3211, 3213, 3079, 3080, 3081, 3082, 3083, 3084, 3085, 3086, 3184, 3185, 3186, 3187, 3037, 3039, 3064, 3062, 3060, 3058, 3056.

Andalusia. 1479+ acres. Re-surveyed for Templeman and McCulloh, 23 January 1840, and patented to Templeman and Stewart, 18 May 1841. Lots: 2268, 2269, 2271, 2282, 2283, 2284, 2286, 2288, 2289, 2270, 2272, 2273, 2264, 2275, 2280, as vacancy 2285.

Aristotle. 200 acres. Re-surveyed for John Brice, 18 July 1831, patented to John H. McFadon, 24 October 1834. Lots: 3224, 3222, 3229, 3228.

Agreement, 159+ acres. Re-surveyed for John Wiley and Christian Beachy, 1 October 1834; patented March 8, 1836. Lots: 2119, 2114, 2116.

Auray, 347+ acres. Re-surveyed for George Templeman, 15 February 1842, and patented to William Grindage, 20 Feb. 1842. Lots: 2722, 2723, 2732.

Alhambra, 255+ acres. Re-surveyed for Templeman and McCulloh, 7 January 1840. Lots: 305, 307, 309, 373, 374.

Alexander the Great, 176+ acres. Re-surveyed for Alexander Sinclair, 3 June 1828, and patented to Alexander Sinclair, 28 September 1840. Lots: 87, 88, 89.

Anvil, 770+ acres. Re-surveyed for John Hoye, 25 Oct. 1838 and patented to John Hoye 28 May 1839. Lots: 473, 475, 476, 477, 478, 479, 480, 481, 482, 483, 486, 488, 489, 490, 491.

Attempt, 200 acres. Re-surveyed for J. G. W. Waters, 23 June 1837, patented to him and C. F. Mayer, 2 May 1838. Lots: 2214, 2215, 2216, 2217.

Addition, 322+ acres. Re-surveyed for Benjamin Stoddert, 15 August 1796; patented to David Hubbard 25 Feb. 1851. Lots: 1860, 1868.

Allegany Republican, 369+ acres. Re-surveyed for Thomas Pollard, 14 February 1812; patented to Edward Armstrong 17 Sept. 1841. Lots: 3552, 3554, 3569.

Apart, 336 acres. Re-surveyed for George Templeman, 6 April 1839; patented to him 4 Dec. 1839. Lots: 3315, 3316, 2869, 2867.

Bridgewater, 364+ acres. Re-surveyed for John Hoye, 20 Sept. 1848 and patented to George Smith, of Alexander, his executor, 19 July 1849. Lots: 3118, 3121, 3124, 3126, 3127, 3129.

Brayton, 71+ acres. Re-surveyed for Richard and Philip H. Bray, 17 July 1830, and patented to them March 3, 1834. Lot no. 284.

Berne, 277+ acres. Resurveyed for Laurence M. Morton and George Templeman, 3 Feb. 1842, and patented to L. M. and M. Morton, 30 Oct 1843. Lots: 224. 301, 306, 308.

Buckdale. Re-surveyed for John J. Ashby, in 1843; not patented. Lots 319, 320.

Bellmont, 100 acres. Re-surveyed for George Calmes, 12 December 1820, and patented to Lucy Perry, 17 March 1841. Lots 1032, 1035.

Bishop's Glebe, 929+ acres. Re-surveyed for J. D. Armstrong, 15 August 1827 and patented to L. A. Armstead, 28 September 1830. Lots 1087, 1088, 1089, 1090, 1091, 1113, 1114, 1115, 1116, 3125, 3128, 3120, 3122, 3123, 3119, 3117, 3115, as vacancy 3116.

Brotherly Love, 150+ acres. Re-surveyed for the heirs of George Lynn, 10 January 1828; patented to them 27 January 1829. Lots, 3012, 3013, 3149.

Bremen, 250+ acres. Re-surveyed for Geo. Templeman and Wm. Morton, 25 January 1842; patented to Wm. Morton, 30 October 1843. Lots 2024, 2026, 2028, 2025, 2027.

Blackstone, 103 acres. Re-surveyed for William Wiland, 19 August 1842, and patented to him 16 June 1843. Lots 2069, 2190.

Brethren in Arms, 199 acres. Re-surveyed for John J. Jacob, 14 June 1830; patented January 29, 1831. Lots 3615, 3616, 3617, 3618.

Brownington, 100 acres. Re-surveyed for Meshack Browning, 7 April 1827; patented February 20, 1834. Lots 1468, 1469,

Brampton, 200 acres. Re-surveyed for John Brice, 15 July 1834; patented to John H. McFadden, 22 Oct 1834. Lots: 1660, 1661, 1662, 1663.

Berry Hill, 104+ acres. Re-surveyed for Jacob Markell, 17 Nov. 1849. patented to him 16 Sept. 1850. Lots 1935, 1972.

Brayton, 102+ acres. Re-surveyed for John Bray, 11 April 1838; patented to him 20 January 1840. Lots: 119, 267,

Bridgeport, 50 acres. Re-surveyed for Templeman and McCulloh, 13 September 1838; patented 22 July 1839. Lot no. 1337.

Burell's Purchase, Re-surveyed for Samuel B. Burell, 17 July 1839 and patented to him 16 May 1840. A re-survey upon *Whetstone Hill.* Re-surveyed *Coal and Ore, Addition to Cook's Adventure. Crinosk's Rushy Run, Coal Land, In Between Hornet's Nest.* Lots 3351, 3352, 3353, 3354, 3355, 3350. *Water Works, Corn's Addition, Trouble for Nothing,* and *Cook's Venture.*

Carrie Fergus, 150 acres. Re-surveyed for Robert Ferguson, 17 May 1848, and patented to him 7 Apr. 1849. Lots 3241, 4143, 4144.

Constance. Resurveyed for Henry Bray, 1 Oct. 1842.; patented to him 23 April 1844. Lot 131.

Cascade, 356+ acres. Re-surveyed for Wm. W. Hoye, 15 August 1827 and patented to John Hoye, 10 November 1829. Lots 1055, 1099, 1098, 1092, 1093, 1094, as vacancy parts of 1094, 1096.

Coal Hill, 144+ acres. Re-surveyed for John Brant, 1 Oct. 1823, and patented to John Brant 18 Oct. 1838. Lots 50, 51, 52.

Cistern. Re-surveyed for John Irons in 1828. Not patented. Lots 206, 207, 208.

Crotia, 452 acres. Re-surveyed for Templeman and McCulloch 2 Jan. 1839, and patented to them 20 April 1840. Lots 353, 354, 355, 361, 362, 363, 364, 365, 366.

Chinese Hut, 101+ acres. Re-surveyed for John Swan, 4 August 1835, and patented to John Swan 16 May 1837. Lots 385, 398.

Civicus, 100 acres. Re-surveyed for George Calmes 13 August 1827 and patented to W. W. Hoye March 10, 1835. Lots 875, 941.

Corunna, 222+ acres. Re-surveyed for Templeman and McCulloh 18 Jan 1840 and patented to Templeman and Stewart 10 May 1841. Lots 1333 and 1336.

Cherry Creek, 1194 + acres. Re-surveyed for John Hoye 18 May 1829 and patented to W. W. Hoye 4 August 1828 [sic]. Lots 2570, 2571, 2572, 1514, 1515, 1516, 1519, 1520, 1521, 1213, 1518, 1207, 1208, 1210, 1211, 1214, 1140, 1145, vacancy 1209, 1215, 1216, 1217, 1218.

Carpenter's Square. Re-surveyed for John Johnson, 28 March 1834, patented to Eleanor Johnson February 24, 1836. Lots 3188, 3189, 1390, 3192.

Carrybaugh, 285+ acres. Re-surveyed for James Chisholm 1 August 1849; patented 7 January 1851; Lots: 1304, 1306, 1302, 1357, 1372.

Clifton. Re-surveyed for the Clifton Coal Company 1 November 1839, patented 24 August 1841. A re-survey of *Coal Pits, Clifton.* Lots 3631, 3632, 3633, 3634, 3635, 4086, 4087, 4089, 4090, part of *Williams Sheep Walk, Air, Snake Den, More Coal, Addition, Evening's Work, Mount Misery, Ridge, Merrillsville, Waddle's Fancy.*

Christian, 350 acres. Re-surveyed for Christian Barkholder, 11 July 1389 [sic; but probably should be 1849) and patented to him 10 June 1851. Lots 2331, 2332, 2333, 2372, 2371, 2373, 2374.

Coromandel, 151+ acres. Resurveyed for John Hoye, 27 Nov. 1838 and patented 26 June 1839. Lots 3778, 3779, 3790.

Christmas Gift, 154+ acres. Re-surveyed for Archibald Thistle, 6 December 1837; patented by him 16 February 1839 for [lots] 2208, 2210, 2211, 2212.

Clementon, 275+ acres. Re-surveyed for Andrew Clements, 25 July 1866 and patented to George Slicer, 14 February 1838. Lots 2736, 2737, 2738, 2739. [Sic. The 1866 date is as originally printed but is probably an error.]

Chalons, 773 acres. Re-surveyed for Richard Drune, 19 April 1838 and patented to him 27 September 1839. Lots 3251, 3248, 3246.

Dorset, 200 acres. James Warren. Certificate, 4 September 1841; patented 28 December 1842. Lots 3191, 4140, 4141, 4142.

Dalecarlia, 219+ acres. Re-surveyed for Templeman and McCulloh 29 September 1838 and patented to Templeman and McCulloh 21 April 1840. Lots 493, 494, 495, 496.

Dundas, 546+ acres. Re-surveyed for John Hoye 8 October 1838 and patented to John Hoye 23 May 1839. Lots 1135, 1136, 1137, 1139, 1142, 1143, 1218, 1504, 1505, 1654, 1655.

Dick's Establishment, 200 acres. Re-surveyed for Michael Wilson 6 April 1826 and patented to him 2 February 1829. Lots 1807, 1817, 1819, 1910.

Drummond, 200 acres. Re-surveyed for John Brice 15 June 1832; patented to John H. McFaden 23 Oct 1834. Lots 1664, 1665, 1680, 1682.

Dairy, 150 acres. Re-surveyed for Stephen Thayer and Lewis Thompson 2 Nov 1827, patented to them 2 Oct 1838. Lot 927, 1023, 1022.

Deep Creek Farm, 851 acres. Re-surveyed for John Hoye 15 Oct 1813, patented 26 January 1815. Lots 1733, 1734, 1736, 1738, 1739.

Euphrata, 50 acres. Re-surveyed for James Swan 4 July 1849 and patented to him 24 October 1849. Lot 113.

Echo, 1296+ acres. Re-surveyed for Jacob Markell 6 July 1848 and patented to him 21 March 1849. Lots 2843, 2848, 2876, 2878, 2880, 2884, 2885, 2886, 2887, 2888, 2889, 2890, 2891, 2892, 2893, 2894, 2895, 2896, 2837, 2842, 2844, 2881, 2882, 2996.

Essline Re-surveyed for Templeman and McCulloh in 1839 and not patented. Lots 274, 275.

Eastern Frontier, 1240+ acres. Re-surveyed for George Calmes 17 May 1827 and patented by Lucy Perry, 17 March 1841. Lots 908, 910, 914, 916, 989, 991, 992, 993, 996, 997, 4040, 4036, 4024, 4025, 4023, 4028.

Elysiansylvania, 901+ acres. Re-surveyed for George Drane and Meshack Browning, 3 September 1832 and patented to John Hoye, 30 December 1843. Lots 1101, 1102, 1150, 1151, 1152, 1153, 1154, 1155, 1156, 1157, 1158, 1159, 1160, 1161, 1162, 1163, 1164, 1104.

Emancipation, 7137 + acres. Re-surveyed for Robert Oliver and James Cunningham and patented to them, 4 August 1830. Lots 1714, 1698, 1702, 1594, 1598, 1600, 1599, 1597, 1595, 1593, 1701, 1699, 1697, 1713, 4154, 1604, 1607, 1609, 1592, 1590, 1588, 1586, 1582, 4155, 1606, 1608, 1591, 1708, 1707, 1706, 1613, 1615, 1625, 1627, 1628, 1630, 1631, 1629, 1626, 1622, 1614, 1612, 3011, 3010, 3009, 1719, 1721, 1723, 1725, 1727, 1731, 3163, 3161, 3159, 3156, 3155, 3157, 3160, 1732, 1728, 1724, 1741, 1741 [sic], 1737, 1735, 1767, 1769, 1771, 1775, 1770, 1768, 1766, 1740, 1742, 1797, 1795, 1793, 1772, 1779, 1778, 1776, 1794, 1796, 1791, 1789, 1781, 3007, 3024, 3926, 3022, 3020, 3018, 3019, 3043, 3041, 3016, 3017, 3014, 3015, 3075, 3076, 3177, 1583, 1584, 1601, 1684, 1108, 1109, 3154, 3153, 3152, 3151, 3150, 3028, 3029, 3167, 3168, 3169, 3170; as vacancy lots, Nos. 1799, 1758, 3001, 3002, 3003, 1718, 1623, 1711, 1709, 1695, 1623, 1111; 5th vacancy lot not numbered.

Echo, 360 acres. Re-surveyed for Templeman and McCulloh 27 January 1843. Lots 2764, 2766, 2767, 2781, 2781, 2783, 2784.

Ex Post Facto. Re-surveyed for John Simpkins 24 September 1812. Patented to Jacob Whilhelm, May 12, 1830. Lots 2814, 2815.

Engrafted Vine, 449+ acres. Re-surveyed for John Hoye 26 December 1826 and patented to George Calmes August 2, 1828. Lots 183, 185, 484, 181, 182, 436, 449, 184.

Elegant Landscape, 150+ acres. Re-surveyed for George Calmes 15 Sept. 1824; patented 2 August 1828. Lots. 2501, 1502, 2503.

Eutaw, 200 Acres. Re-surveyed for Templeman and McCulloh, 23 September 1838; and patented by them 9 Jan. 1840. Lots: 2304, 2306, 2308, 2309.

Enfield, 309+ acres. Re-surveyed for John Hoye 8 October 1838; patented 25 May 1839. Lots 2535, 2536, 2538, 2540, 2541, 2542.

Fog, 104+ acres. Re-surveyed for James McGirr, 4 January 1840 and patented by him 26 February 1845. Lots 23 and 24.

Fayette. Re-surveyed for Catharine Townshend 3 November 1841, under 20 years possession, and patented to her 21 February 1848. Composed of lots 1498, 1671, 1676, 1678, originally awarded to Capt. Samuel McPherson.

Francisco, 182 acres. Re-surveyed for Jacob Markell 6 February 1849 and patented to him 29 November 1849. Lots 2558, 2559, 2560.

Fox Range. Re-surveyed for Jacob Markell, 27 July 1848 and patented to him 21 March 1849. Lots 290, 283, 284.

Factories. Re-surveyed for George W. Devecmon, 19 December 1838; patented to the Union Manufacturing Company, 30 March 1840. Lots: 71, 72, 73, 28, 29, 30, 31, 32, 33, 38, 45, 47, includes as vacancy nos. 43, 44, 46, 39, 35, 34, 74.

Flamborough. Re-surveyed for John Hoye _ _ 1828 and patented to John Hoye June 8, 1832. Lots: 99, 178.

Fairfield. Re-surveyed for James Swann 20 June 1829 and patented to James Swan February 8, 1832. Lots: 280, 281, 282, 285.

Flavia, 354+ acres. Re-surveyed for James Smith 5 January 1838 and patented to John Hoye 7 September 1838. Lots: 1226, 1229, 1230, 1231, 1232, 1235 (1225 as vacancy).

Feik's Farm, 517+ acres. Re-surveyed for John Feike 5 August 1805; patented to him February 22, 1825. [It] is a re-survey on a tract called *Bad is the Best of it*. Lots: 2821, 2822, 2823, 2824, 2825, 2826, 2827.

Fathers, Son and Brothers, 310+ acres. Re-surveyed for Robert Greene and William Broadwater 7 October 1826 and patented January 17, 1831. Lots: 2523, 2524

Fairlie Park, 607+ acres. Re-surveyed for James Cunningham 10 January 1831; patented to him and Robert Oliver, 8 May 1832. Lots: 2391, 2392, 2393, 2419, 2420, 2417, 2418, 2379, 2380, 2381, 2382.

Falls of Muddy Creek, 541+ acres. Re-surveyed for Wm. Lynn, 14 August 1827 ; patented March 2, 1837. Lots: 1260, 1261, 1262, 1265, 1266, 1256, 1258, 1263, 1264, 1269.

France, 200 acres. Re-surveyed for John Frantz, of Joseph, 19 December 1836; patented to him 15 March 1851. Lots: 2765, 2776, 2775, 2768.

Fatherland, 633+ acres. Re-surveyed for Jacob Markell 7 November 1849; patented 6 September 1850. Lots: 1953, 1909, 1942, 1859, 1847, 1815, 1811, 1860, 1944, 1809.

Flowery Vale, 973+ acres. Re-surveyed for David Lynn, 28 July 1797 and patented to Abraham Fleckinger 15 November 1828. A resurvey on *Accident.* Lots: 3345, 3346, 3347, 3348.

Guinea. Re-surveyed for Wilmore Neale, 21 February 1842, and patented to him 6 June 1844. Lot: 131.

Good Luck. Re-surveyed for George C. Perry, 1851; not patented. Lots: 981, 4045.

Goodly Luck, 603+ acres. Re-surveyed for David Lynn, 6 September 1830 and patented to F. A. Schley and others, 22 June 1839. Lots: 1237, 1238, 1239, 1240, 1241, 1242, 1244, 1246, 1248, 1250.

Gonton, 94+ acres. Re-surveyed for John Gon, 15 November 1842; patented by him 25 June 1844. Lots: 2579, 2486

Glen Eyry, 4624 acres. Re-surveyed for R. Oliver and J. Cunningham 13 June 1829 and patented to them August 6, 1830. Lots: 2087, 2089, 2085, 2083, 2039.

Greece, 200 acres. Re-surveyed for John Brice, 17 July 1831; patented to John H. McFadon, 23 October 1834. Lots: 1457, 1458, 1459, 1460.

Geneva, 109 acres, 15 perches. Re-surveyed for John Devecmon and Anna Maria Armstrong, 6 February 1850; patented to them 5 November 1850. *Geneva* contains Lots: 4157. 4158, 1711, 1712, 4156, 1709, 1710, 1695, 1696, 1603, 1605, 1703, 1704, 1610, 1611, 1587, 1589, 1585.

Good Meadows, 25 acres. Re-surveyed for Gen. John Swan, 27 May 1799 and patented 30 Dec. 1800. A re-survey on *Rich Glade* and lots 1233 and 1236.

Good Prospect, containing 200 acres; patented to Thomas S. Alexander, 1840, sold to Jacob Pixel, 1851. Lots: 3180, 3181, 3182, 3183.

Glade Farm, containing 718 acres. Re-surveyed for John Hoye, 28 July 1813; patented June 17, 1816. Lots: 830, 831, 847, 848, 850, 856, 860, 867.

Hunter, containing 3364+ acres. Re-surveyed for James W. McCulloh and George Templeman, 3 January 1840, and patented to George Templeman and David Stewart, 19 July 1842, embracing lots :1096, 1079, 1081, 1083, 1085, 1076, 1078, 1080, 1082, 1069, 1067, 1065, 1063, 1061, 1064, 1062, 1059, 1049, 1053, 1046; 1048, 1050, 1052, 1054, 1037, 1035, 1033, 1031, 1029, 1027, 1034, 1032, 1026, 807, 817, 820, 821, 822, 823, 824, 834, 835, 836, 4164, 987, 985, 983, 988, 984, 982, 980, 913, 915, 917, 880, 926, 1097, 1077, 1072, 1060, 1058, 1057, 1056, 1024, as vacancy nos. 1051, 1055, and 1028.

Hoye's Last Hope. Re-surveyed for John Hoye, 1 January 1839, and patented to him 20 August 1839, embracing Lots: 12, 92, 93, 94, 95.

Harrison, containing 2,794+ acres. Re-surveyed for Templeman and Stewart, 31 Dec. 1839 and patented to Templeman and McCulloh, 4 June 1841. Lots: 895, 896, 897, 898, 899, 901, 902, 920, 1914, 1916, 1825, 1840, 1836, 1837, 1875, 1184, 1169, 1182, 1170, 1187, 1188, 1172, 1183, 1179, 1189, 1178, 1174, 1147, 1146, 4029, 4031, 4032, 4033, 4034, 4035, 4036, 4027, 4043, 4037, 4038, 4042, 4044, 4046, 4048, 4049, 4051.

Hunter's Dale, containing 561+ acres. James Cunningham, 20 August 1827; patented 7 Aug. 1828. Lots: 2421, 2422, 2424, 2426, 2398, 2369, 2370, vacancy 2367, 2368, 2396, 2395.

Huron, 200 acres. Re-surveyed for John Brice, 19 June 1830; patented to John W. McFaden, 23 July 1831. Lots: 2836, 2737, 2738, 2739.

Hampton, 401+ acres. Re-surveyed for John Hoye, 26 Oct 1833; patented December 4, 1836. Lots: 1734, 1736, 1738, 1739, 1798, 799, 3004, 3005.

Henry's Lots, containing 100 acres. Re-surveyed for Henry Waltz, 10 March 1826; patented September 18, 1827, Lots: 1205, 1206.

Inheritance, 250+ acres. Re-surveyed for heirs of Robert Cresap, 9 Jan. 1828 and patented to S. Cresap and others 25 February 1829. Lots: 1196, 1197, 1198, 1199, 1200.

Ithica, 750 acres. Re-surveyed for McCulloh and Templeman, 10 January 1840, and patented to Templeman and Stewart, 23 March 1841. Lots: 1546, 1548, 1549, 1550, 1551, 1552, 1553, 1556, 1557, 1559, 1560, 1561, 1562, 1563, 1564.

Ington, 200 acres. Re-surveyed for John Brice, 19 July 1831; patented to John H. McFadon, 24 October 1834. Lots: 2728, 2729, 2730, 2731.

Internal Improvement, 5,832+ acres. Re-surveyed for John B. Armistead, 20 December 1831; patented to John B. Armistead and Gen. Walker K. Armistead, 24 April 1834. Lots: 2429, 2431, 2441, 2442, 2445, 2446, 2448, 2449, 2450, 2451, 2452, 2453, 2454, 2455, 2456, 2457, 2460, 2461, 2462, 2463, 2464, 2465, 2466, 2467, 2468, 2469, 2470, 2471, 2472, 2473, 2478, 2479, 2480, 2481, 2482, 2483, 2484, 2485, 2488, 2489, 2490, 2492, 2491, 2492, 2493, 2494, 2495, 2573, 2575, 2676, 2577, 2578, 2583, 2584, 2585, 2588, 2593, 2594, 2660, 2664, 2668, 2669, 2670, 2671, 2672, 2673, 2674, 2675, 2691, 2692, 2693, 2694, 2697, 2721, 2724, 2725, 2726, 2727, 2733, 2735, 2740, 2741, 2742, 2743, 2744, 2745, 2746, 2748, 2749, 2750, 2751, 2752, 2753, 2754, 2755, 2756, 2757, 2762, 2763, vacancy nos.: 2477, 2474, 2475, 2427, 2447, 2444, 2443, 2439, 2700, 2703, 2658, 2659, 2663, 2667, 2635, 2634, 2632.

Jonathan and Saul, 633+ acres. Re-surveyed for Jonathan Wilson, 7 January 1828, and patented to him 20 March 1847. Lots: 1902, 1921, 1883, 1176, 1177, 1175, 1149, 1166, 1843, as vacancy, 1148.

Jaffa, 335+ acres. Re-surveyed for George Templeman, 30 Dec. 1841 and patented to William Morton 20 October 1843. Lots: 75, 77, 78, 180, 314, 315.

John Hoye's Wish, 303+ acres. Re-surveyed for John Hoye 14 May 1839 and patented to him 18 March 1840. Lots: 225, 227, 229, 231, 230, 234.

Junius. Re-surveyed for James Swan, 5 August 1835, and patented to James Swan, 16 May 1837. Lots: 450 and 451.

Jutting Roof, 108+ acres. Re-surveyed for John Hoye 14 Dec. 1826; patented to George Calmes, 10 April 1828. Lots: 1221, 1222.

Jepso, 200 acres. Re-surveyed for John Brice, 19 July 1831; patented to John H. McFadon, 22 October 1834. Lots: 1660, 1661, 1662, 1663.

Java, 606+ acres. Re-surveyed for George Templeman, 26 May 1840; patented to Templeman and Grindage, 25 Aug. 1841. Lots: 4136, 3271, 3272, 3273.

Jewelry, 702+ acres. Re-surveyed for Wm. Jewell, 10 Feb. 1840; patented to Wm. Jewell and George Templeman 11 Oct. 1841. Lots: 1490, 1496, 1497, 1675, 3087, 3091, 3092, 3093, 3094, 3095, 3096, 3097, 3195.

Killington, containing 214 acres. Re-surveyed for Meshack Browning, 10 April 1827; patented to him, May 1, 1829. Lots: 1479, as vacancy, 1473, 1475, 1478, 1473.

Knickerbocker, containing 996+ acres. Re-surveyed for Templeman and McCulloh, 11 January 1840 and patented to Templeman and Stewart 12 March 1841. Embracing Lots: 2080, 2082, 2086, 2090, 2092, 2093, 2094, 2095, 2096, 2097, 2098, 2099, as vacancy, 2037.

Kensington, containing 201+ acres. Re-surveyed for John Brice, 11 June 1830 and patented to John W. McFadon, 23 July 1831. Lots: 2970, 3138, 2972, 3139.

Lupo, 100 acres. Re-surveyed for Jacob Markell, 11 July 1848; patented to him, 21 March 1849. Lots: 2975, 2979.

Leonidas, 1,215+ Acres. Re-surveyed for Henry Naylor, 25 January 1839 and patented to him 12 August 1856. Lots:

1117, 1118, 1119, 1120, 1123, 3133, 3132, 3130, 3131, 3108, 3110, 3112, 3114, 3116, 3109, 3101, 3113, 1649, 1646, 1644, 1642, 1640, 1641, 1643.

Lynn's Lots, containing 196+ acres. Re-surveyed for David Lynn, 18 May 1825 and patented to him 29 December 1825. Lots: 1529, 4055.

Lorraine, containing 600 acres. Re-surveyed for George Templeman and Bennet Clements, 25 January 1842; patented to Bennet Clements 16 August 1842. Lots: 2359, 2360, 2361, 2362, 2363, 2364, 2365, 2366, 2387, 2388, 2389, 2390.

Littleton, containing 205+ acres. Re-surveyed for Eli Ridgely, 12 May 1835 and patented to him 3 March 1838. Lots: 2209, 2213, 2262, 2263.

Latent Worth, containing 10,761 acres. Re-surveyed for Oliver and Cunningham 15 June 1829 and patented to them 23 August 1830. Lots: 1992, 1993, 1994, 1997, 1998, 1936, 1937, 1995, 1990, 1934, 4159, 1999, 1974, 1982, 1979, 1971, 1983, 1973, 1985, 1970, 1969, 1978, 1975, 1966, 1967, 1976, 1977, 1965, 1964, 2000, 2001, 2002, 2003, 2004, 2005, 2006, 2007, 2008, 2009, 2012, 2035, 2034, 1959, 1960, 1961, 1954, 1955, 1957, 1956, 1948, 1951, 1949, 1980, 1981, 1987, 1988, 1886, 1887, 1945, 1946, 1947, 1888, 1889, 1917, 1884, 1885, 1940, 1941, 1952, 1943, 1897, 1898, 1812, 1848, 1846, 1872, 1873, 1871, 1870, 1813, 1810, 1800, 1802, 1803, 1816, 1867, 1869, 1833, 1818, 1804, 1805, 1806, 1820, 1831, 1832, 1829, 1822, 1821, 1827, 1824, 1823, 1826, 2036, 2032, 1962, 1968, 4th vacancy is parts of lots 1989, 1918, 1919.

Leatherwood, contains 150+ acres. Re-surveyed for John Hoye 10 Sept. 1835, patented 12 June 1836. Lots: 1476, 4113, 4115.

Limestone, 1,239 acres. Re-surveyed for Gen. John Swan, 10 May 1799, patented 29 December 1800. Re-survey on the *Cove, Yough Meadows,* Lots: 1474, 1475, 1476, 1499, 1492, 1479, 1480, 4100, 4101, 4102, 4103, 4105, 4106, 4107, 4108, 4109, 4110, 4111, 4112, 4114, 4116.

Luck Valley, 617+ acres. Re-surveyed for William Hilleary; patented 7 January 1815. *Venture, Walnut, Hollin and Luck,* lots: 3543, 3539, 3540.

Markelton, 1029+ acres. Re-surveyed for Jacob Markell, 13 July 1847 and patented to him 21 November 1848. Lots: 1828, 1843, 1845, 1853, 1854, 1855, 1874, 1877, 1928, 1930, 1932, 1849, 1838, 1882, 1899, 1905, 1907, 1126.

Moon's Vexation or *Mount Vexation,* 187+ acres. Re-surveyed for William Harvey 7 January 1839 and patented to him 24 January 1848. Lots: 413, 395, 494.

Mecklenburg, 860+ acres. Re-surveyed for Templeman and McCulloh, 2 October 1838 and patented 20 April 1840. Lots: 161, 162, 163, 133, 134, 152, 153, 136, 150, 151, 154, 156, 158, 159, 144, 140, 138.

Montgomery, 207+ acres. Re-surveyed for George Gaither, 25 March 1836, and patented to Ephriam Gaither 26 February 1844. Lots: 3266, 3233, 3234, 3337.

Mill Seat. Resurveyed for ...., and patented to John Miller, ... 1830. Lots: 347, 348, 349, 313.

Megara, 351+ acres. Re-surveyed for Templeman and McCulloh, 2 January 1840 and patented to Templeman and Stewart 10 May 1841. Lots: 371, 369, 377, 390, 452, 455, as vacancy, 450.

Meteor, 250+ acres. Re-surveyed for Templeman and McCulloh, 14 February 1840 and patented to Stewart and Templeman 2 June 1847. Lots: 409, 410, 411, 412, 414.

Mt. Gilboa, 150 acres. Re-surveyed for John Davis 27 June 1838 and patented to John Davis 22 August 1839. Lots: 429, 433, 434.

Memphis, 475 acres. Re-surveyed for J. Hoye, 27 May 1830 and patented to W. W. Hoye, 27 March 1833. Lots: 829, 830, 381, 832, 833, 856, 1028, 1029, 1031.

Montrose, 111+ acres. Re-surveyed for McCuloh and Templeman 17 January 1840, and patented to Templeman and Stewart 10 March 1841. Lots: 1254, 1259.

Modena, 254+ acres. Re-surveyed for Lawrence M. Morton and Richard W. Templeman, 24 January 1842, and patented to them 30 Oct. 1843. Lots: 1890, 1891, 1895, 1896, 2033.

Medelpadia, 2,127 acres. Re-surveyed for McCulloh and Templeman, 21 January 1840 and patented to Templeman and Stewart 16 September 1841. Lots: 1282, 1283, 1284, 1293, 1295, 1404, 1405, 1407, 1408, 1410, 1411, 1412, 1414, 1416, 1417, 1418, 1419, 1420, 1422, 1431, 1432, 1433, 1434, 1435, 1436, 1437, 1441, 1442, 1443, 1444, 1445, 1449 1450, 1451, 1452, 1453, 1462, 1446, 1447, 1463, as vacancy 1421, 1461.

Muddy Creek, 565+ acres. Re-surveyed for Oliver and Cunningham, 10 June 1829 and patented August 7, 1830. Lots: 1271, 1272, 1276, 1280, 1270, 1273, 1274, 1270, 1273, 1274,1277, 1278, 1279, as vacancy, 1281.

Meadow Mountain Glade, 645 acres. Re-surveyed for James Cunningham 22 August 1829; patented 29 April 1828. Lots: 2014, 2016, 2021, 2023, 2013, 2015, 2018.

Meadow Mountain, 467+ acres. Re-surveyed for Francis Thomas, 8 September 1849; patented to Jacob Markell, 24 September 1850. Lots: 2040, 2041, 2081, 2084.

Montevue, 322+ acres. Re-surveyed for Jacob Markell, 6 February 1849; patented 16 March 1850. Lots: 2520, 2521, 2522.

Naylorsville, 151+ acres. Resurveyed for Henry Naylor, 24 Jan 1851; patented 10 November 1851. Lots: 1121, 1122, 1131.

Neponset, 187+ acres. Re-surveyed for Joseph and Moses Glass, 29 October 1849 and patented to them 7 July 1851. Lots: 3271, 3272, 3273.

Nova Zembla. Re-surveyed for James McGin, 28 February 1838, and patented to J. McGirr, 5 March 1840. Lots: 84, 179.

Nest Lick, 706+ acres. Re-surveyed for George Calmes, 17 May 1827; patented to Lucy Perry, 17 March 1841. Lots: 1073, 1100, 1105, 1107, 1103, 1175, 1708, 1706, 1707, 1585 and 1589, as vacancy, nos. 1074, 1705, part of 1772.

Norwood's Farm. Escheated by Samuel Norwood in 1799 and patented in 1801. Lots: 3615, 3616, 3617, 3618.

New Year, 250 acres. Re-surveyed for Jacob Markell, 1 January 1851; patented 12 August 1851. Lots: 2024, 2025, 2026, 2027, 2028.

Outlot, 50 acres. Re-surveyed for John Beekman, 14 November 1849 and patented to John Beekman, 22 September 1850. Lot: 352.

Ox Pasture, 795+ acres. Re-surveyed for J. Hoye, 10 September 1835; patented 7 December 1836. Lots: 1892, 1893, 1894.

Partnership, 352+ acres. A re-survey on lots 3856, 3929, 3845, 3846, 3927, 3928, *Sugar Camp* and *How Can That Be* re-surveyed for James Pearcy and John Cowan, 16 June 1848; patented to them 18 February 1851.

Pine Glade, 125+ acres. Re-surveyed for Jacob Markell, 5 December 1849; patented 6 September 1850. Lots: 1950, 1963.

President Jefferson, 250 acres. Re-surveyed for Jefferson Broadwater, 16 May 1839; patented to him 19 February 1840. Lots 3882, 3883, 3884, 3885, 3896.

Pluto, 200 acres. Re-surveyed for Templeman and McCulloh, 25 January 1840, and patented to Templeman and Stewart 7 May 1841. Lots: 3099, 4147, 4118, 1677.

Paradise, 650+ acres. Re-surveyed for Wm. W. Hoye, 30 August 1830 and patented 7 June 1832. Lots: 495, 1319, 1316, 1315, 1314, 1301, 1359, 1360, 1361, 1362, 1350, 1351, 1351, 1352.

Plains of Bear Creek, 862+ acres. Re-surveyed for Clement Smith, 10 January 1828; patented to Harrison Black, March 2, 1836. Lots: 3066, 3067, 3068, 3069, 3070, 3071, 3031, 3034, 1340, 3042, 3044, 3047, 3033, 3054, 3052, 3050, 3165 as vacancy.

Potomac Manor, 10,794+ acres. Re-surveyed for Gen. John Swan, 16 May 1799, patented 24 December 1800. Resurvey on

Both Ends of the Bush, Both Ends of the Bush and Sugar Tree Bottom United, Forwarning, Sugar Tree Bottom, Cocklefield, Deer Park, The Prices, and Lots: 432, 433, 425, 157, 137, 125, 126, 121, 114, 119, 249, 129, 100, 111, 112, 118, 272, 279, 276, 269, 255, 256, 240, 90, 251, 252, 241, 242, 244, 245, 246.

Pretty Prospect, 305+ acres. Re-surveyed for Henry Mattingley, 17 July 1796; patented to Lewis Howell, 15 September 1838. Lots: 4077, 4078, 4079, 3666, 3667.

Pembroke, 90+ acres. Re-surveyed for Isaac McCarty, 29 September 1848, and patented to him, 29 November 1849. Lots: 2558, 2559, 2560.

Patmos, 100 acres. Re-surveyed for James Swan, 5 July 1839, patented to him, 24 October 1849. Lots: 110, 114.

Pelican, 736+ acres. Re-surveyed for Thos. Wilson, Sr., and Thos. Wilson, Jr., 30 April 1834 and patented to Thos. Wilson, Sr., 15 --- 1836. Lots: 368, 372, 374, 396, 397, 420, 421, 423, 424, 426, 375, 376.

Parents and Child, 105 acres. Re-surveyed for Wm. White, 1 March 1825 and patented to him 29 December 1825. Lots: 1529, 4055.

Pinto, 100+ acres. Re-surveyed for Elie Swearingen, 21 February 1842, and patented to him 24 February 1843. Lot 3570.

Quinquagesima, 1,228+ acres. Resurveyed for George Templeman, 5 November 1842; patented to Templeman and Edward A. Dickins, 24 July 1844. Lots: 3035, 3036, 3038, 3051, 3053, 3055, 3057, 3063, 3065, 3073, 3074, 3077, 3078, 3179, 3226, 3227, 3230, 3232, 3234, 3235, 3236, 3239, 3240, 4151.

Richard the Third, 600 acres. Re-surveyed for Richard Drane, 1 January 1834 and patented to Edward Johnston and John M. Carleton, March 20, 1841. Lots: 3603, 3604, 3605, 3606, 3607, 3608, 3609, 3610, 3611, 3612, 3613, and 3614.

Roanoke, 450 acres. Re-surveyed for Eli Ridgely, 15 May 1833; patented October 25, 1834. Lots: 2330, 2336, 2327, 2328, 2329, vacancy, 2322, 2323, 2324, 2325.

Rhinoceros, 645+ acres. Re-surveyed for Templeman and McCullough, 24 October 1838, and patented to them, 19 December 1839. Lots: 166, 168, 169, 171, 172, 173, 175, 176, 177, 400, 401, 407, 408.

Reform, 150 acres. Re-surveyed for Samuel Friend, 29 June 1850 and patented to him 11 November 1851. Lots: 1051, 1066, 1068.

Rainy Season, 289 acres. Re-surveyed for Nicholas Friend, 21 March 1826, patented to Frederick Claus, 24 Apr. 1829. This tract was taken upon vacancy by special warrant; is composed of Lots: 1745, 1747, 1748, 1794, 1716.

Salem, 400 acres. Re-surveyed for John Beachy, 27 April 1850; patented to him 9 January 1851. Lots: 2352, 2352, 2354, 2355, 2356, 2357, 2358.

Sacramento, 200 acres. Re-surveyed for Jacob Markell, 19 November 1849; patented to him 10 February 1851. Lots: 1190, 1191, 1175, 1177.

Sandy Spring, 247+ acres. Re-surveyed for Jacob Markell, 6 Dec. 1849, patented 11 October 1851. Lots: 2088, 2091, 2037.

Senior and Junior, 293+ acres. Re-surveyed for Thomas Wilson Senior, and Junior, 18 April 1835; patented to them 4 February 1837. Lots: 122, 135, 147.

Sierra Nevada, 100 acres. Re-surveyed for Jacob Markell, 3 December 1949 [sic., prob. should be 1849], patented to him 16 September 1850. Lots: 1894 and 1986.

San Marino, 245+ acres. Re-surveyed for John Hoye, 3 December 1837, patented to John Hoye, 22 November 1838. Lots: 800, 813, 825, 837, 869.

Sweet Alley, 221 acres. Re-surveyed for George Calmes, 18 May 1827, patented to Lucy Perry, 17 March 1841. Lots: 903, 995, and 4041, vacancy, no. 904.

Sextile. Re-surveyed for and patented to Templeman and McCulloh, --- ---, 1840. Lots 427, 428, 429, 430, 431, 433.

Spa, 203+ acres. Re-surveyed for James Swan, 4 August 1835 and patented to James Swan, 15 May 1837. Lots: 399, 400, 402, 403.

Scales, 405+ acres. Meshach Browning, 9 June 1829, patented to him 1 February 1830. Lots: 1288, 1290, 1296, 1297, 1298, 1299.

Scotia, 100 acres. Re-surveyed for Archibald Chisholm, 2 November 1826, and patented to him, 11 February 1835. Lots: 1138, 1140.

Scott's Lessons, 300 acres. Re-surveyed for David Scott, 24 March 1834; patented 13 April 1835. Lots: 3093, 3094, 3095, 3096, 3097, 3098.

Security, 158+ acres. Re-surveyed for Henry Naylor, 2 August 1849, and patented to him, 1 May 1850. Lots: 1124, 1125, 1130.

Sharp Practice. Re-surveyed for John A. Smith, ----, and patented to Henry Naylor, ---1851. Lot: 1134.

Shepherd's Tent, 656+ acres. Re-surveyed for W. W. Hoye, 15 July 1831, patented June 6, 1832. Lots: 1565, 1570, 1571, 1572, 1573, 1574, 1775, 1576, 1577, 1673, 1492, 1490, vacancy, 1674.

Siege of Acre, 1,831+ acres. Re-surveyed for Templeman and McCulloh, 27 August 1838 and patented to Templeman and Stewart, 4 December 1839. Lots: 1153, 1154, 1155, 1156, 1157, 1159, 1161, 1162, 1101, 1102, 1150, 1104.

Skeleton, 107+ acres. Re-surveyed for Samuel Van Buskirk, 14 December 1826; patented to him 3 January 1827. Lots: 3721.

Summit Point, 255+ acres. Re-surveyed for Jacob Markell, 3 November 1849, and patented to him, 11 February 1851. Lots: 1875, 1184, 1185, 1186, 1168.

Summer Retreat, 700 acres. Re-surveyed for George Calmes, 21 March 1822, patented to him ---. Lots: 807, 820, 821, 822, 823, 824, 834, 835, 836, 4164, 987, 985, 983, 984.

Summer Retreat Enlarged, 353+ acres. Re-surveyed for George Calmes, 23 March 1822; patented to him, 4 February 1824. Lots: 1024. 1025, 1026, 1027, 1054, 1056, 1057.

Spikerton, 200 acres. Re-surveyed for Solomon Spiker, 14 November 1842; patented to him 15 May 1815 [sic]. Lots: 2711, 2712, 2713, 2714.

Sulphuric Springs, 500 acres. Resurveyed for Holmes Wiley, 6 July 1849; patented 14 October 1850. Lots: 2310, 2311, 1215, 2316, 2318, 2307, 2305, 2302, 2303.

Shandy Hall, 838+ acres. Re-surveyed for General John Swan, 10 May 1799; patented 30 December 1800, Lots: 30, 41, 42, 34, 35, 36, 37, 38, 40, 83, 253.

Squirrel Range, 187+ acres. Re-surveyed for Leonard Smith, 31 May 1836, patented to him 12 February 1839. Lots: 2945, 22949, 2960, 2962.

Sweet Pink, 201+ acres. Re-surveyed for Templeman and McCulloh, 21 September 1838; patented to them 19 December 1839. Lots: 2983, 2984, 2985, 2986.

Tecumseh, 199+ acres. Re-surveyed for William Drane, 30 July 1840; patented to him 21 October 1841. Lots: 3254, 3255, 3256, 3257.

Test, 209+ Acres. Re-surveyed for Wm. Jewell, 10 February 1840; patented to Wm. Jewell and George Templeman, 11 October 1841. Lots: 1485, 1486, 1488, 1495.

Thanet, 600 acres. Re-surveyed for George Templeman and Bennet Clements, 24 January 1842; patented to Wm. Morton, 28 Oct. 1843. Lots: 2127, 2144, 2146, 2147, 2110, 2111, 2143, 2145, 2148, 2149, 2150, 2151.

Thessalia, 350+ acres. Re-surveyed for Templeman and McCulloh, 25 September 1838, and patented to Templeman and McCulloh, 28 December 1839. Lots: 291, 292, 294, 295, 297, 298, 299.

The Plains, 725+ acres. Re-surveyed for Gen. John Swan, 27 August 1799, patented 30 December 1800. Re-survey on lots 367, 370, 382, 384, 386, 387.

The Wilderness Shall Smile, 200 acres. Re-surveyed for Edward McCarty, of Isaac, 28 February 1825; patented to him 9 February 1826. Lots: 864, 865, 871, 937.

The Land of Nod, 1060+ acres. Re-surveyed for James D. Armstrong, 17 Sept. 1831, patented to Wm. W. Hoye, May 12, 1835. Lots: 1685, 1691, 1693, 1694, 1686, 1688, 1689, 1690, 1692.

The Green Meadows of Deep Creek, 1408+ acres. Re-surveyed for Clement Smith, 29 August 1626 [sic, prob. 1826], patented to John A. Smith, 15 April 1833. Lots: 1844, 1922, 1924, 1925, 1926, 1927, 1929, 1931, 1128, 3101, 3102, 3103, 3104, 3105, 3107, 1763, 1761, 3100, 1760, 1762, 1645, 1646, 1647, 1648, 1903, 1904, 1127, 1129, 1133.

The Gleanings of Negro Mountain, 400 acres. Re-surveyed for Wm. Stanton and John H. Ridgely, 15 April 1849; patented to them 9 July 1850. Lots: 2347, 2348, 2349, 2350, 2343, 2344, 2345, 2346.

Triumph, 878+ acres. Re-surveyed for J. Hoye, 24 October 1834, and patented by John Hoye, 13 December 1836. Lots: 381, 456, 457, 458, 459, 460, 462, 464, 471, 474, vacancy, 466, 467, 454, 380, 379.

Tuame, 199+ acres. Re-surveyed for J. Hoye, 21 March 1836; patented to Mary Ann and Marone Drane, 1 July 1837. Lots: 3344, 3331, 3340, 3262.

Turkey Lodge, 177+ acres. Re-surveyed for William Broadwater, 9 October 1826; patented by him, 5 February 1840. Lot: 3895

Two in One, 100 acres. Re-surveyed for Henry White, 19 May 1827, patented to him 10 October 1829. Lots: 418, 419.

Twineine, 100 acres. Re-surveyed for Thos. Wilson, 12 April 1827 and patented 23 February 1829. Lots: 138, 140.

Ultramarine, 100 acres. Re-surveyed for Jacob Enlow, 11 October 1828, patented March 6, 1833. Lots: 3316, 3317.

Uncleton, 945+ acres. Re-surveyed for Samuel Hoye, 13 August 1827; patented 4 August 1828. Lots: 1193, 1194, 1195, 3134, 1900, 1901, 1908, 1881, 1863, 1865, 1938, 1939, 1864, 1862, 1861, 1857, 1856, vacancy, 3106.

Underwald, 150+ acres. Re-surveyed for Benedict Miller, 25 December 1828, patented January 15, 1831. Lots: 2124, 2126, 2078.

Underdorff, 159 acres. Re-surveyed for Elizabeth H. Hoye, 31 December 1828, Patented to Wm. W. Hoye, May 8, 1833. Lots: 1464, 1466, 1467.

Utica, 199+ acres. Re-surveyed for Upton Bruce, 14 Oct. 1828, and patented to Robert Bruce and others, March 26, 1833. Lots: 2954, 2955, 2956, 2957.

Veronica the Nun, 955+ acres. Re-surveyed for J. Hoye, 16 May 1827 and patented to Wm. W. Hoye, 4 August 1828. Lots: 1040, 1042, 1045, 839, 826, 827, 815, 802, 1038, 1036, 1039, 1044, 1047, 1070, vacancy, 837, 825, 201, 1041, 1043.

Virginia Frontier, 878+ acres. Re-surveyed for W. W. Hoye, 24 January 1831; patented June 8, 1832. Lots: 323, 324, 325, 326, 328, 329, 330, 332, 333, 334, 335, 336, 337, 338, 339, 343, 344.

Wayne, 163+ acres. Re-surveyed for James W. McCulloh and George Templeman, 16 January 1840 and patented to Templeman and D. Stewart, 19 March 1841. Lots: 1245, 1247, 1252.

Western Canal Convention, 1454+ acres. Re-surveyed for J. Hoye, 24 August 1826; patented to William W. Hoye, August 14, 1827. Lots: 859, 878, 879, 881, 812, 944, 844, 952, 1002, 1007, 950, 1006, 949, vacancy, 882, 942, 1001, 883, 943, 879, 867, 946, 954, 1004, 955, 887, 947, 972.

Whetstone's Lots, 190+ acres. Re-surveyed for Samuel and Daniel Whetstone, 23 March 1839, and patented to Samuel and Jacob Whetstone, 5 March 1841. Lots: 2964, 2966, 2068, 3137.

White's Hospitality, 668+ acres. Re-surveyed for J. Hoye, 1826 and patented to W. W. Hoye, 4 August 1828. Lots: 212, 218, 220, 221, 222, 209, 195, 223, 210, 192, 193, 194, 190, 191, 303, 304.

Winston, 1452+ acres. Re-surveyed for W. W. Seaton, 8 December 1846; patented to him, 6 September 1850. A re-survey on *Smith's Farm, Smith's Addition,* and Lots: 1390, 1338, 1384, 1391, 1396, 1382, 1383.

Willamette, 205 acres. Re-surveyed for Jacob Markell, 5 November 1849. Patented 6 September 1850. Lots: 1912, 1713, 1914, 1916.

White Plains, 4175 acres. Re-surveyed for David Lynn, 25 September 1826, and patented to him 15 December 1827. Lots: 1141, 1512, 1513, 1543, 4053, 4054, 4056, 4058, 4059, 4060, 2554, 4066, 2553, 2556, 2557, 4065, 959, 961, 962, 964, 965, 967, 968, 969, 970, 971, 977, 1009, 1010, 1101, 1014, 1015, 1016, 1017, 1018, 1019, 1020, 1500, 1501, 1502, 1503, 1506, 1507, 1508, 1509, 1510, 1511, 1522, 1530, 1532, 1537, 1538, 1539, 1541, 1531, 4047, 4050, 4052, 4062, 863, 870, 873, 925, 930, 934, 936, 939, 1534, 1535, 1536, 1544, 2544, 2545, 2546, 2547, 2548, 2549, 2552, vacancy, 2543, 1523.

Williamsburg, 355+ acres. Re-surveyed for Wm. W. Hoye, 23 May 1827, patented June 23, 1831. Lots: 1493, 1494, 1489, 3172, 3173, 1491, 1487.

Western Territory, 239+ acres. Re-surveyed for Wm. W. Hoye, 10 August 1827; patented 23 June 1831. Lots: 4098, 4099, 1483, 1484.

Workman's Farm, 112+ acres. Re-surveyed for Isaac Workman, 5 December 1804; patented to The Boston and New York Coal Company 21 March 1838. Lots: 3656, 3657.

William and Mary, 932+ acres. Re-surveyed for Wm. W. Hoye, 3 July 1833, and patented to James Smith, 4 December 1838. Lots: 1387, 1389, 1322, 1329, 1395, 1331, 1323, 1330, 1379, 1380, 1381, 1374, 1375, 1376, 1377, 1354, 1378, 1363.

Westphalia. Re-surveyed for Israel Thompson, 6 April 1826, and patented to Israel Thompson, 6 March 1832. Lots: 957, 889.

Woodbury, 155+ acres. Re-surveyed for McCulloh and Templeman, 7 January 1840, and patented to Templeman and Stewart, 23 March 1841. Lots: 296, 383, 406.

Wilderness, 200 acres. Re-surveyed for Michael Wilson 6 April 1826; patented to him 5 February 1829. Lots: 387, 388, 389, 391.

Wing, 148+ acres. Re-surveyed for J. Hoye, 8 November 1826, patented to Wm. W. Hoye, August 4, 1828. Lots: 316, 317, 318.

Zenith, 100 acres. Re-surveyed for George Loar, 18 June 1829; patented to George Loar, 25 February 1833. Lots: 923, 929.

ADDENDA

The following is transcribed in toto from The Laws of Maryland, December session, 1825: Resolution 66, passed by the Legislature 3 March 1826:

"Whereas, Terrane [sic] Doyle, became the purchaser of lot number 346, westward of Fort Cumberland, who paid for the same, 2 December 1794, and assigned his right to the said lot to Luke Maloney, who on the 8th September 1808, obtained a patent: and whereas, by mistake and inadvertance of the then register of the land office, a proclamation warrant was issued to Robert Sinclair, to resurvey and ... the said lot, who assigned the same to Peter Devicman, who assigned the same to John Templeman, and the said John Templeman had the same resurveyed, and a certificate thereof returned to the land office on 6 September 1796, paid to the treasurer of the western shore the sum of 12 pounds ten shillings for caution, and 5 shillings for improvements, and on the 9th day of July 1801, obtained a patent for the same. Therefore,

"Resolved, That the treasurer of the western shore pay to John Templeman or to his order the sum of $34.00, with interest thereon from 6 September 1796, out of any unappropiated money in the treasury, to reimburse him the sum paid into the treasury, on 6 September 1796 as a proclamation warrent to resurvey and affect lot number 346, west of Fort Cumberland, in Allegany county; which warrant issued improperly by the then register of the land office of the western shore."

For further information on "Internal Improvement" see the published Laws of Maryland 1832: Chapter 18 and Resolution 25.

REVOLUTIONARY PENSIONERS OF THE STATE OF MARYLAND

Abbott, George - 1/2 pay of a Pvt. 1812:36

Adams, Adam - 1/2 pay of a Pvt. 1815:35

Alcock, Robert - of AA co., Md, 1/2 pay of a Pvt. 1828:7

Alexander, Mary - wid. of Jacob, 1/2 pay of a Sgt., during her widowhood. 1835:24

Allen, Jacob - 1/2 pay of a Pvt. 1812:56

Allen, Nathan - of QA co., MD, 1/2 pay of a Pvt. 1833:14

Alvey, Josias - of StM co., Md, 1/2 pay of a Pvt. 1815:25

Amos, Elizabeth - of BA City, 1/2 pay of a Capt. 1833:44
    Pay balance to Samuel B. Hugo, of BA, heir of Elizabeth Amos, deceased. 1839:31

Anderson, John - 1/2 pay of a Pvt. 1817:51

Anderson, Richard - 1/2 pay of a Capt. in the Maryland Line, for disability acquired in the service. 1785: Chapter 17

Auld, Daniel - of TA co., MD, 1/2 pay of a Pvt. 1825:102
    Pay to Sarah Auld, wid. of Daniel, such sum of money due Daniel at his death. 1831:35
    Pay to Sarah Auld of TA co., MD, wid. of Daniel, 1/2 pay of a Pvt. 1831:84
    Pay to Philip Pasterfield, legal representative and surviving brother of Sarah Auld, wid. of Daniel, deceased (28 June 1847) bal. due. 1847:10

Ayres, Elizabeth - wid. of Thomas, 1/2 pay of a Pvt. 1836:13

Baily (Bayley), Mountjoy - to receive five full years pay of a Capt. in lieu of 1/2 pay for life as compensation for his services during the Revolutionary War. 1810:2
    Register of the Land Office to issue to Mountjoy Baily, a warrant for 200 a. of land in AL co., MD. 1825:25

Baily, Thomas - 1/2 pay of a Pvt. 1818:78

Gambrill, Maria - wid. of Henry Baldwin, 1/2 pay of a Lt. 1830:30
    Pay bal. due, (2 mos.) to Maria Gambrill, decd., to her son, William H. Baldwin of AA co., Md. 1835:38

Baker, Henry Cleland - late a Lt. in the 3rd MD Regt., deprived of the use of his limbs probably from being exposed in several campaigns in SC in Continental service; to receive 1/2 pay of a Lt. which will be charged to the U.S. 1791:Res.

Baldwin, Samuel - 1/2 pay of a Pvt. 1835:33

Baltzel, Jacob - the name, Jacob corrected to Charles 1801:3. See June 21, 1797

Bantham, Peregrine - of KT co., MD, 1/2 pay of a Pvt. 1816:51

Barrett, Joshua - 1/2 pay of a Sgt. as relief from the indigence and misery which his attend his decrepitude and old age. 1804:13

Barrott, Solomon - 1/2 pay of a fifer. 1815:15
    Pay to wid., Susan Barrott. 1852:Chapt. 348

Bateman, George - 1/2 pay of a Corp. 1815:9

Bayley, Mountjoy - Pay balance due him as a Major Commandant of Militia and guard over British prisoners in 1781 and 1782 at Frederick-town, FK Co. 1790:Res.

Beall, Henrietta - wid. of Lawson Beall, 1/2 pay of a Pvt. 1839:16

Beall, Lloyd - 1/2 pay of a Capt. 1815:27
    To wid., Elizabeth, 1/2 pay of a Capt. 1817:7

Beall, Maj. William D. - 1/2 pay of a Maj. 1808:Res.

Bean, Leonard - of Mason co., KY, 1/2 pay of a Pvt. 1831:99

Semmes, Anne, of Georgetown, DC, widow of Thomas Beatty, 1/2 pay of a Lt. 1832:66

Beatty, Jane - of Pittsburgh, PA, 1/2 pay of a Lt. 1826:72

Beaven, Charles - of HA co., MD, "an old Revolutionary Officer," 1/2 pay of a Lt. 1815:26

Beck, Simon and William Usselton, soldiers of the Revolution to be paid a sum not exceeding $50.00 for support and maintenance. 1822: Chapt. 90

Beckwith, Nehemiah - of DO co., Md, 1/2 pay of a Pvt. 1826:24

Becroft, John - of BA co., MD, "an old Revolutionary Soldier", 1/2 pay of a Pvt. 1816:33

Belt, John Sprigg - 1/2 pay of a Capt. in the MD Line in lieu of the $125.00 allowed him by 1811:36. 1815:8

Bennett, Frederick - of DO co., Md, "an old Revolutionary Soldier," 1/2 pay of a Corp. 1811:54

Bennett, John - 1/2 pay of a Pvt. 1816:37

Benson, Joseph - 1/2 pay of a Pvt. 1856:77

Benson, Perry - 1/2 pay of a Capt. for disability acquired in the service in the MD Line... 1785: Chapt. 17
    Pay to Mary Benson, wid. of General Perry Benson, 1/2 pay of a Capt. 1829:52

Berry, Edward - soldier of the Revolution, received a grant of 52+ a. in AL co., MD, and was said to have d. without heirs and the land was escheated to the state; this resolution gives relief to Robinson Savage, Jr. of AL co. for the land, called *Cricket Legs*. 1831:38

Bewley, Grace - Widow of George Bewley, pay $200.00 arrears of pension due her husband, Pvt., 1/2 pay of a Capt. 1858: Chapt. 245

Bidwell, Richard - of BA city, 1/2 pay of a Pvt. 1816:38

Bishop, Jane - wid. of Leonard Ennis (q.v.), 1/2 pay of a Pvt. 1837:10

Blake, John - of WO co., MD, 1/2 pay of a Pvt. 1825:58
    Patsy Blake, wid. of John, of WO co., MD, 1/2 pay of a Pvt. 1833:48

Bluer, James - of FK co., Md, 1/2 pay of a Pvt. 1831:77

Bolton, John - 1/2 pay of a Pvt. 1812:66

Bomgardner, William - of WA co., MD, 1/2 pay of a Pvt. 1819:50
    Pay to wid., Margaret Bomgardner of WA co., MD, 1/2 pay of a Pvt. 1826:29

Bond, John - of Hampshire co., VA (now WV), 1/2 pay of a Sgt. 1825:59

Boone, John - of CH co., MD, a Lt. , $125.00 annually. 1811:57
    Boone, John - 1/2 pay of a Lt. in lieu of the sum already allowed him. 1815:7

Bowen, Jehu - Late Lt. in the Maryland Line, did as an Ensign receive a wound...to receive payment to be charged to the U.S. 1788:8

Bowers, George - 1/2 pay of a Pvt. 1836:28

Boyer, Michael - 1/2 pay of a Capt. 1816:32

Bracco, Bennett - Pay to heir at law of Capt. Bracco Bennett of TA co., MD, $250.00 in lieu of 200 a. of bounty land. 1838:48

Branson, John B. - 1/2 pay of a Pvt in his indigent situation and advanced years. 1812:34
    Pay balance $12.11, due, to widow, Mary of StM co., MD and 1/2 pay of a Pvt. beginning 1 Jan 1840. 1839:12

Brashears, Ignatius - an old soldier of PG co., MD, 1/2 pay of a Pvt. 1817:19

Brewer, Susanna - of Annapolis city, wid. of Thomas Brewer, 1/2 pay of a Sgt. 1823:23

Brewer, Thomas S. - of Annapolis city, 1/2 pay of a Sgt. 1812:20

Brice, Julianna, widow, 1/2 pay of a Lt. 1832:64

Britt, Robert, late soldier in Capt. Dorsey's Company; John Sheredine, late a soldier in the 1st Maryland Regt.; and Roger

Skiventon, late soldier in Capt. Ford's Company, depreciation pay to be liquidated. 1790: Res.

Britton, Joseph - of Hawkins co., TN, 1/2 pay of a Lt.; Joshua Burgess of Mason co., KY; and Robert Wilmot of Bourbon co., KY, all granted 1/2 pay of Lts. 1829:12 (N.B. Britton's name is given in one instance as George.)

Brooks, Elizabeth - of HA co., Md, widow of Joshua Rutledge, 1/2 pay of a Lt. 1839:13

Bruce, Robert - "an old Revolutionary soldier", 1/2 pay of a Pvt. 1816:36

Bruce, Robert - of CH co., MD, 1/2 pay of a Trooper instead of a common soldier in the line as allowed by the last session of the Legislature. 1817:17

Bruce, William - 1/2 pay of a Capt. in the Maryland Line. 1812:19

Bruff, James - 1/2 pay of a Capt. for service in the Maryland Line, wounded and disabled. 1785: Chapt. 17
    Bruff, Margaret, of QA co., widow of James, 1/2 pay of a Capt. 1819:8

Bryan, Charles - of Lycoming, co., PA, 1/2 pay of a Pvt. 1826:34

Bryant, James - of QA co., Md, 1/2 pay of a Pvt. 1840:15

Bullock, Jesse - 1/2 pay of a Pvt. in the Maryland Line. 1812:27

Burch, Benjamin - of KY, 1/2 pay of a Pvt. 1827:42

Burgess, Basil - 1/2 pay of a Lt. 1816:20

Burgess, Joshua - of Mason co., KY, 1/2 pay of a Lt. 1829:12

Pay to Nicholas D. Coleman, attorney for heirs of Joshua Burgess, $46.70, bal. due at time of death. 1835:6

Burgess, Vachel - 4 years full pay as a Captain, free from interest, as compensation for service in the Revolutionary War. 1810:6

Burk, Nathaniel - of BA City, 1/2 pay of a Pvt. 1828:64
    Pay to Elizabeth, wid. of Nathaniel Burk of BA city, 1/2 pay of a Pvt. 1837:23

Burns, John - 1/2 pay of a Pvt. 1818:70

Burroughs, Eleanor Turner - of StM co., Md, wid. of Norman Burroughs, 1/2 pay of a Pvt. 1838:35

Busey, Anne - sole legatee of Benjamin Topham, deceased, late a pensioner of this state to be paid arrears of Topham's pension. 1838:50

Bush, Joseph - of TA co., MD, 1/2 pay of a Pvt. 1819:23

Butt, Edward, soldier in the 2nd MD Regt. was killed in action at Guildford Court House 16 Mar. 1781; Back pay of 86 lbs, 18 sh. to be paid to one of his representatives, Thomas Butt. 1787:Res.

Byas, William - of DO co., MD, 1/2 pay of a Boatswain. 1820:65
    Byas, William - above Resolution rescinded and new resolution passed granting him 1/2 pay of a Lt. 1819:43
    Byus, William - of DO co., MD, pay bal. due to heirs. 1858:175

Cadle, Ann - legal representative of Richard Hall, decd., to be paid $17.60, amount due at time of his death. 1840:3

Cahoe, Thomas - of CH co., MD, 1/2 pay of a Pvt. 1812:44

Callahan, Sarah, of Annapolis, wid. of John Callahan, 1/2 pay of a 1st Lt. 1838:36

Campbell, George - to be placed on pension list of the State. 1800:1 (This resolution does not state whether or not Campbell was a soldier. However, an alphabetical listing of invalid Pensioners compiled in 1822, notes Campbell was a Pvt.)

Canfield, Thomas - enlisted as a Pvt. in the 4th MD Regiment in 1781 and served in the MD Line until the end of the war; he was employed as a labourer to the workmen on the Stadthouse; on 12 Nov. last he fell from the roof of the Stadthouse and was much injured and was carried home senseless; he is in a languishing condition and unable to support himself, his wife and two helpless children. The Justices of AA county Orphans Court are to make him an allowance the same as a maimed and disabled soldier while he continues unable to support himself. 1786: Res.

Carlin, Mary - wid. of William Carlin, 1/2 pay of a Pvt. 1836:55

Carney, Thomas - 1/2 pay of a Pvt. 1811:33

Carr, Hezekiah - 1/2 pay of a Drummer in the Maryland Line. Extra Session, 1813:3

Carr, Ingram - 1/2 pay of a Pvt. 1812:51

Carr, John - To be paid 5 years full pay as a Lt. as commutation of 1/2 pay of a Lt. 1810:16

Loney, Margaret - formerly Margaret Carr, of BA co., MD, wid. of John Carr, 1/2 pay of a Pvt. 1845:53
    Above Resolution repealed and new resolution passed correcting the widow's name to Margaret Long. 1846:7

Carvin, James - late soldier in the 4th Maryland Regt. to be issued liquidation certificate for depreciation pay. 1791:Res.

Casson, Philip - of Caroline co., 1/2 pay due him as a disabled officer of the U.S. 1790:Res.
    Pilip Casson - of Caroline co., 486 lbs. for half pay due him as a disabled officer from 22 Dec. 1778 to 22 Dec. 1795 plus 1/2 pay of an officer for life or until he is placed on the pension list of the U.S. 1796:Res.

Cato, George - 1/2 pay of a Pvt. 1818:73

Chambers, Edward - of AA co., MD, "A man of colour", 1/2 pay of a Pvt. 1819:34

Chapman, Henry H. - of Georgetown, DC, 1/2 pay of a Lt. 1819:38
    Chapman, Mary - wid. of Henry H. Chapman, of Georgetown, DC, 1/2 pay of a Lt. 1832:60

Chapman, Thomas - of DO co., Md, 1/2 pay of a Pvt. 1823:30

Charlton, John Usher - to receive 187 lbs, 18s, due him as depreciation pay as Paymaster of the 4th Maryland Regt. from 24 April to 1 Oct 1778. 1798:Res.

Chesley, Capt. Robert - late of StM. co., a warrant to be issued to his heirs for 200 a. of land in AL co., MD. 1827:39

Clagget, Ami - wid. of Dr. Samuel Clagget, 1/2 pay of a Surgeon's Mate. 1833:52

Clarke, James 1/2 pay of a Matross for "relief from his indigence which attend his decrepitude and old age." 1812:53
    Pay to Barbara McMahon, formerly wife of James Clarke 1/2 pay of a Pvt., also pay $21.66, the amount due Clarke at his death. 1849:65

Clewley, Joseph - of MT co., MD, 1/2 pay of a Pvt. 1815:37
   Pay bal. due ($11.11) to Henry Harding for use of Mary Wheland, his legal heir. 1829:14

Clinton, Thomas - 1/2 pay of a Fife Major. 1812:43

Cochran, James - Pay to Capt. James Cochran, of CE co., Md, $200.00 as compensation for services during the Revolutionary War. 1822:59

Cochrane, James - 1/2 pay of a Pvt. 1836:21
   Pay to wid., Ann Mary, of FK co., MD, 1/2 pay of a Pvt. 1846:20

Coe, Richard - of PG co., MD, 1/2 pay of a Sgt. 1829:33
   Register of the Land Office to issue warrant and patent to Richard Coe of PG co., MD, for 50 a. in AL co., MD. 1831:32
   Pay to George C. Coe, son of late Richard Coe, of PG co. $30.00 as so much as was due the said Richard at his death. 1843:30

Coe, William - of BA co., MD, 1/2 pay of a Pvt. 1819:39
   Resolution 1819:39, rescinded. William Coe, now of Annapolis, is to receive 1/2 pay of a Pvt. of Matross. 1820:30
   Pay to Mary Coe, wid. of William Coe, $12.50, amount due her husband at time of his death. 1833:39
   Pay Mary Coe, wid. of William Coe, 1/2 pay of a Matross. 1833:39
   Pay to Alexander Benson Coe, $50.00, the amount of 1 yrs. pension, due Mary Coe, at the time of her death. 1834:2

Coffroth, Conrad - of Franklin co., PA, 1/2 pay of a Fifer. 1825:69

Pay to Magdalena Coffroth, wid. of Conrad, now of WA co., [MD or PA?], 1/2 pay of a Pvt. 1831:81

Colegate, Asaph - 1/2 pay of a Pvt. 1841:44

Coleman, Patten - of BA co., MD, now upward of 65 yrs. of age; served 6 yrs. in the Revolutionary War; wounded in the thigh which occasions him to halt in this member; petitions the Assembly for support. Support granted. 1803:78

Connelly, Hugh, Sr. - of WA co., MD, 1/2 pay of a Pvt. 1816:15

Connelly, Priscilla - wid. of William Connelly, 1/2 pay of a Pvt. 1831:46
 Pay balance due Priscilla to her dau. Priscilla. 1854:267

Cooke, Henry - 1/2 pay of a Pvt. 1834:4

Cooper, William - of Ohio co., KY, 1/2 pay of a Pvt. 1831:95
 A warrant/patent to be issued to Cooper, for 50 a. of land in WA co., MD at no cost... 1831:98

Courts, Eleanor C. - of PG co., MD, wid. of Dr. Richard Hanley Courts, 1/2 pay of a Surgeons Mate. 1820:42

Coward, Nancy - wid. of William Coward, 1/2 pay of a Lt. 1852:292

Coyn, Dominick - of HA co., MD, 1/2 pay of a Pvt. 1803:15
 To Mary Coyn of HA co., wid. of Dominic Coyn, 1/2 pay of a Pvt. 1823:33

Cox, James - in BA-town Militia, fell in the cause of American freedom in action at Germantown...left a wid., Mary Cox and children unprovided for; she to receive 1/2 pay of a Major. 1788:22

Cox, William - 1/2 pay of a Pvt. 1803:101

Crampton, Thomas - 1/2 pay of a Pvt. 1834:61

Crawford, Nehemiah - 1/2 pay of a Sgt. 1816:41

Cresap, Joseph - 1/2 pay of a Lt. 1818:41
  Resolution rescinded as he is said to be living in affluence. 1821:62
  Re-instated; Joseph is of AL co., MD; he has a large family. 1825:67

Croft, Catharine - wid. of William Croft, 1/2 pay of a Corp. 1834:71

Cross, Mary - wid. of Robert Cross, 1/2 pay of a fifer. 1854:255

Crouch, Robert - 1/2 pay of a Pvt. 1812:32
  Pay Hannah Crouch of CE co., wid. of Robert Crouch, $11.33 due her husband at his death. He received his pension up to 2 July 1823 and d. 12 Oct. next. 1844:13

Croxall, Charles - of BA city, 1/2 pay of a Capt. of Dragoons. 1826:59
  Pay to Claudius LeGrande, $31.67, bal. due at death of Charles Croxall. 1831:82

Curtis, John - of BA city, 1/2 pay of a matross in the Artillery. 1828:30

Davidson, James - 1/2 pay of a Pvt. 1816:28

Davis, John - of CH co., MD, 1/2 pay of a Sgt. 1812:49

Davis, Margaret - wid. of Samuel 1/2 pay of a Pvt. 1834:66

Davis, Samuel - of KT co., MD, 1/2 pay of a fifer. 1819:37
    Davis Samuel, drummer and William Gudgington, a Pvt., both of KT co., MD, both on the pension list were never in service of the state or the U.S.; stricken from the pension list. 1822:65

Davis, Samuel - of BA co., 1/2 pay of a Sgt. 1825:104
    Samuel Davis - of BA city, to be paid pension accruing from the time he was stricken from the list until he was replaced thereon... 1828:66

Davis, Thomas - of OH, 1/2 pay of a Pvt. 1819:31

Davis, William - 1/2 pay of a Pvt. 1816:21

Dawkins, Elizabeth - of CT co., MD, wid. of the late Charles Dawkins, 1/2 pay of a Sgt. 1829:59

Dawson, Capt. Joseph - in the 5th MD Regt. in service of the U.S., is disabled from wounds received at the Battle of Eutaw Springs, and at times is incapable of getting a livelihood to receive 1/2 pay he received in continental service and it is to be charged to the U.S. 1791:Res.
    Dawson, Joseph - to be paid 9 lbs, 57s, 6p, in lieu of a lot of land due him as a soldier in the 5th MD Regt. 1793:Res.

Dawson, William - of CE co., MD, "A 'meritorious soldier' 1/2 pay of a Pvt. in his indigent situation now advanced in life." 1810:Res.

Deal, George, Capt. - Deceased. Pay bal. due to Richard Thomas. 1842:5

Deaver, Aquilla - of HA co., MD, 1/2 pay of a Pvt. 1826:27

Pay bal. due at death ($6.66) to William B. Stephenson, for use of Sarah Deaver, wid. of Aquilla. 1835:14.
Pay to wid., Sarah Deaver, 1/2 pay of a Pvt.
Petition of Julia Ann Harwood of HA co., only surviving child and heir of Sarah Deaver states that Sarah d. 24 Nov. 1850 and there was due her from the state $15.85. Sarah owed John H. Mitchell a sum of money therefore pay balance due Sarah Deaver at her death to Mitchell. 1852: Chapt. 349

Deaver, William - of Mason co., KY, 1/2 pay of a Pvt. 1825:84

DeKalb, Baron - Resolution urging U.S. Congress to pay heirs compensation. 1851:8

Dennis, Edward - a soldier in the 3rd Maryland Regt., granted a Depreciation Certificate. 1796:Res.
    Edward Dennis - 1/2 pay of a Pvt. 1835:69

Denny, Augusta - wid. of Capt. Robert Denny, 1/2 pay of a Capt. 1814:20

Denoon, John - of OH, 1/2 pay of a Drummer. 1828:36

Dent, Eleanor - wid. of John Dent, 3rd Regt., Maryland Line, 1/2 pay of a Pvt. 1834:49

Dent, George - of StM co., MD, 1/2 pay of a Pvt. 1828:9

Dixon, William - 1/2 pay of a Pvt. 1818:21

Donally, Patrick - of FK co., MD, 1/2 pay of a Pvt. 1815:22
    Pay bal. due at death to wid., Elizabeth. 1828:23
    Pay Elizabeth Donnelly of FK co., wid. of Patrick Donnelly, 1/2 pay of a Pvt. 1831:69

Dorgan, John - of TA co., MD,, 1/2 pay of a Pvt. 1827:2

Dorrent, John - a soldier in the 7th Maryland Regt.; Andrew Hagerty, a soldier in the 6th Maryland Regt., and the legal representative of James Quay of the lst Maryland Regt. to receive certificates of depreciation. 1790:Res.

Dorsey, Ely - of Ely, of FK co., MD, $960.00 full payment for his services in the Revolutionary War. [Rank not given] 1818:61

Dorsey, Richard - Late Capt. in the Artillery from MD, in service of the U. S., disabled from wounds received at the Battle of Camden, SC, and is unable to earn a sustenance, the Governor of Maryland to grant him 1/2 pay of what he received in Continental service and the same to be charged to the U. S. 1791: Res.

Dotrow, John - of FK co., MD, 1/2 pay of a Pvt. 1827:45

Downing, Nathaniel - of PG co., MD, 1/2 pay of a Pvt. 1817:22

Due, James - 1/2 pay of a Pvt. 1818:71

Duffee, Thomas - of HA co., MD, 1/2 pay of a Sgt. 1819:25
    Pay to Bridget, wid. of Thomas Duffee, 1/2 pay of a Sgt. 1834:15
    Pay to James Moore, for use of Bridget Duffee, wid. of Thomas Duffee, of HA co., amount due him at his death. 1834:37

Dunning, Butler - of CH co., MD, 1/2 pay of a Pvt. 1820:40
    Pay bal. due at death (18 Nov. 1829) to widow, Elizabeth Downing. 1832:21
    Elizabeth Downing - wid. of Butler Downing, 1/2 pay of a Pvt. 1834:29

Duval, Joseph - of MT co., MD, an old Revolutionary soldier, 1/2 pay of a Pvt. 1820:39

Duvall, Benjamin - of Elisha, an old Revolutionary soldier, 1/2 pay of a Pvt. 1821:32
    Pay to Benjamin L. Gantt, executor of Benjamin Duvall, of Elisha, who d. 30 Jan. 1830, bal. due for use of Benjamin Duvall, Jr.1829:21

Dyer, Walter - 1/2 pay of a Lt. 1816:9

Easton, Sarah - who was the wid. of John Jordan, 1/2 pay of a Capt. 1835:26

Ebbs, Emanuel - 1/2 pay of a Pvt. 1815:48

Edelin, John - pay to Walter H. S. Mitchell, his administrator, $12.00 bal. due Edelin at his death. 1837:11

Edgerly, Capt. Edward - Officer in the Maryland Line, fell in service leaving no legal representative but had a natural son whom he acknowledged, a young child to be named Edward Edgerly who is to receive the interest due from the State and the U.S. to Capt. Edgerly, until he becomes age 21 yrs. or marries when he is to receive the full amount. Daniel Ramsay appointed guardian. 1782: Chapt. 49.

Eisell, John - of BA, 1/2 pay of a Pvt. 1831:83

Elliott, Robert - of HA co., "a wounded Revolutionary Soldier" 1/2 pay of a Pvt. in the Maryland Line. 1811:26

Elliott, Thomas - an "old" Revolutionary Soldier, 1/2 pay of a Pvt. 1812:45

Elliott, Thomas - of BA, 1/2 pay of a Pvt. 1826:30

Ellis, Michael - of Craven co., NC, 1/2 pay of a Fifer. 1825:112.

Elliss, Thomas - of HA co., MD, 1/2 pay of a Pvt. 1820:48

Emory, Charles - an old Bargeman, who has 7 lbs. due him for services on board barges during the Revolutionary War. [No rank given] 1801:9

Bishop, Jane - who was the wid. of Leonard Ennis, 1/2 pay of a Pvt. 1837:10

Evans, Thomas - of FK co., 1/2 pay of a Pvt. also a warrant for 50 a. in AL co., MD. 1829:64
    Pay to Eleanor, widow of Thomas Evans, of FK co., 1/2 pay of a Pvt. 1833:41

Ewing, James - 1/2 pay of a Capt. for service in the Maryland Line; wounded, maimed and disabled. 1785:17.

Fairbrother, Francis - of AA co, 1/2 pay of a Pvt. 1806:Res.
    Pay to wid., Patience, of AA co., 1/2 pay of a Pvt. 1831:72

Fearson, Joseph - 1/2 pay of a Pvt. 1815:32

Fennell, Stephen - of Brown co., OH, 1/2 pay of a Pvt. 1832:36

Fickle, Benjamin - of Muskingum co., OH, 1/2 pay of a Lt. 1826:23

Fitzgerald, Benjamin - of KY, 1/2 pay of a Quartermaster Sgt. 1833:50

Fitzgerald, Nicholas - of WA co., MD, 1/2 pay of a Pvt. 1819:36

Fitzhugh, Capt. William - of CT co., 1/2 pay of a Capt. "on the British establishment" from 3 Sept. 1783 to 1 Nov. 1791 with interest. 1791:10

Fitzpatrick, Nathan - 1/2 pay of a Pvt. 1839:23

Fling, James - of MT co., 1/2 pay of a Sgt. 1823:27
    Pay to Henry Harding , executor of James Fling, now decd; for use of James W. Fling, $7.00, balance due. 1836:11

Fogget(t), Richard - of AA co., 1/2 pay of a Pvt. 1819:35
    Pay to Arthridge, wid. of Richard Foggett, balance due him at his death. 1834:72
    Pay to Arthridge, wid. of Richard Foggitt, 1/2 pay of a Pvt. 1834:65
    Pay to order of legal representatives, balance due Arthidge Fogget arrears in pension due her on 20 May 1849 from 1 Jan, 1849 in lieu of above. 1849:27
    Pay to Gassaway Owens, legal representative of Arthridge Foggett, arrears in pension. 1849:31

Ford, Hezekiah - of CE co., MD, 1/2 pay of a Lt. 1821:20

Ford, Mary - wid. of Joseph, 1/2 pay of a 2nd Lt. 1836:33

Forest, Mrs. Rebecca - pay bal. due her at time of death to Ann Green and Maria Bohrer, sole surviving children. 1843:17

Fox, Anthony - of AA co., 1/2 pay of a Sgt. 1806:Res.

Frazier, Henrietta M. - of BA city, wid. of William Frazier, 1/2 pay of a Lt. 1839:7

Frazier, James - of DO co., an old soldier, 1/2 pay of a Pvt. 1819:21

Pay to Susan Frazier, bal. of pension due to James Frazier at the time of his death and that pension paid to James be continued to be paid to Susan Frazier. 1846:31

Frazier, Levin - of DO co., an old Revolutionary officer, 1/2 pay of a 1st Lt. 1819:32
Pay to Elizabeth, of DO co., wid. of Levin Frazier, 1/2 pay of a Lt. commencing 5 July 1842; also pension due her husband at his death. 1842:2
Pay to Priscilla Jackson, legal representative of Elizabeth Frazier, $8.00, balance due Elizabeth at time of her death. 1847:51
Pay Samuel Harrington, trustee of the late Elizabeth Frazier $18.22, amount due her at her death. 1849:51

Frazier, Samuel - of HA co., 1/2 pay of a Pvt. 1816:6
Pay to Penelope, wid. of Samuel Frazier, 1/2 pay of a Pvt. 1835:70
Pay to Priscilla Frazier, executor of Penelope Frazier, of BA co., sum due her estate at the time of her death, December 2, 1848. 1849:7

Frazier, Solomon - 1/2 pay of a Capt. 1818:80
Pay Solomon Frazier, Capt., $337.75, balance due him for rations while in service of the state of MD during the Revolutionary War, with interest from 1 Jan. 1819. 1821:21

Gadd, Thomas - 1/2 pay of a Pvt. 1811:10

Gallaher, John - late soldier in the 6th MD Regt., to be paid 61 lbs 1s 5d, depreciation pay due for services as a soldier. 1798:8

Galworth, Gabriel - of MT co, 1/2 pay of a Pvt. 1816:14

Gambell, Abraham - soldier in 1st MD Regt.; wounded through the shoulder at Camden, 1 Apr. 1781, Is unable to support himself, granted so much money as with what he receives from the U.S. will equal 1/2 pay he received in continental service and to be charged to the U.S. 1791:Res.

Gambrel, Gideon - of CA co., , 1/2 pay of a Pvt. 1826:25

Gassaway, Henry - of AA co., 1/2 pay of a Lt. 1804:Res.

Gassaway, John - 1/2 pay of a Capt. 1815:17
    Elizabeth L. Gassaway, of Annapolis, widow of John Gassaway, 1/2 pay of a Capt. 1819:15

Gassaway, Gen. John - To be paid $600.00, the difference between the pay of officers of his rank and what he actually was paid. 1817:59
    Pay to Elizabeth L. Gassaway, wid. of Gen. John Gassaway, $38.00 due on his pension at his death. 1821:4

Gates, William - 1/2 pay of a Pvt. 1815:33

Gerrish, Edward - 1/2 pay of a Pvt. 1812:56

Gibbart, Peter - pay $200.00 full compensation for services in the Revolution. 1815:31

Gilpin, William - of Jefferson co., VA [now WV], 1/2 pay of a Pvt. 1826:26

Goddard, John - of PG co., 1/2 pay of a Pvt. 1828:29
    Pay Raphael C. Edelin $16.89, for use of Benjamin Goddard, of PG co, only child...of John Goddard who d. 2 Sept. 1831. 1832:3

Godman, Capt. Samuel - Land Office to issue warrant for 200a of land westward of Ft. Cumberland in AL co. to representatives of. 1856:2

Goldsborough, Charles - 1/2 pay of a Pvt. 1815:34

Goldsborough, Ann - of StM. co., 1/2 pay of a Pvt. 1833:62

Goldsmith, Thomas - Register of the Land Office to issue a warrant for 200 a. of land westward of Ft. Cumberland, AL co., to James, Thomas, and Elizabeth Mills; Sarah Campfield, and Harriet Goldsmith, heirs of Thomas Goldsmith, deceased... 1835:46

Gomber, John - of FK co., 1/2 pay of a Pvt. 1824:26

Gordon, Archibald - of CE co., a meritorious soldier in the Revolutionary War, 1/2 pay of a Pvt. 1807:Res.

Gordon, Elizabeth - widow of John Gordon, 1/2 pay of a Pvt. 1820:41

Gould, Sarah - of DO co., widow of William Gould, 1/2 pay of a Pvt. 1829:21

Gray, George - of CH co., 1/2 pay of a Pvt. 1819:41

Green, Elizabeth - widow of Henry Green, 1/2 pay of a Pvt. 1849:61

Greentree, Benjamin - of MT co., 1/2 pay of a Pvt. 1819:24
    Mary Greentree - of FK co., widow of Benjamin, $10.00 for quarterly pension due him at his death and pay her 1/2 pay of a Pvt. 1839:15
    Pay to Elizabeth Beall, any money due Mary Greentree at the time of her death. 1847:14

Griffin, Nathan - of DO co., an old soldier, 1/2 pay of a Pvt. 1816:35

Griffith, Philemon - and old Revolutionary officer, 1/2 pay of a Major. 1818:57

Griffith, Samuel - 1/2 pay of a Capt. 1818:64
    Pay to Ruth, widow of Samuel Griffith, of MT co., amount due her husband at time of his death. 1833:18

Grove, David - of WA co., 1/2 pay of a Pvt. 1819:54
    Pay Catharine Grove, wid. of David, 1/2 pay of a Pvt. 1831:54
    Pay bal. due to David Brookhart for the use of Catharine Grove, wife of David Grove, amount due her said husband at the time of his death. 1831:55

Grove, Mary - wid. of William Grove, late of AL co.,1/2 pay of a Pvt. 1849:47
    Pay balance due (1/4 of his pay) to wid., Mary Greentree of FK co. 1849:15 (see below)

Groves, William - of AL co., 1/2 pay of a Pvt. 1819:30 See above.

Gudgeon, William of KT co., "an old soldier", 1/2 pay of a Pvt. 1818:68
    Gudgeon, William of KT co., 1/2 pay of a Pvt and also the sum presently due him. 1823:21
    Gudgeon, William - Pay to representatives, money which may be due him at his death. 1827:11

Gudgeon, William - pay to Benjamin Gudgeon, one of the heirs of William, decd., amount due him at his death. 1828:22

Gwyn, Julia - wid. of John Gwinn, 1/1 pay of a Sgt. 1836:54

Hafley, Stephen - of FK co., Md , 1/2 pay of a Pvt. 1829:31
    Pay to John B. O'Boyle for use of Mary M., wid. of Stephen, Hafley, bal. due him at his death ($31.22). 1838:13
    Pay wid., Mary Magdalena, 1/2 pay of a Pvt. 1838:15

Halkerstone, Robert of CH co., Edward Tillard of MT co., John McCoy, John S.[prigg] Belt, Gassaway Watkins, Cornelius H. Mills, and John J. Jacob, each to be paid the sum of $125.00 annually. 1811:36

Halkerson, Robert - of CH co., Md., 1/2 pay of a Lt. instead of sum allowed him by Resolution of 6 Jan. 1812 [1811:36]. 1817:20 See below.

Hall, Richard - of AA co., MD, 1/2 pay of a Pvt. 1831:17

Hammond, Elizabeth - of FK Co., 1/2 pay of a Pvt. 1843:33

Hamilton, Margaret, of BA city, MD, widow of John A. Hamilton, 1/2 pay of a Capt. 1823:34

Handy, Elizabeth - widow of George Handy, 1/2 pay of a Capt. 1837:13
    Pay Anne G. Handy, executrix of Elizabeth Handy, late of SO co., MD - balance due ($54.00). 1837:14

Handy, Nancy, wid. of Capt. Levin Handy, late of SO co., Md, 1/2 pay of a Capt. 1821:19

Woolford, Priscilla, of SO co., MD, former widow of Isaac Handy, 1/2 pay of a Pvt. 1837:29

Haney, Wm. - Pay wid., Susanna Haney of BA city, MD, 1/2 pay of a Pvt. 1838:61

Hanson, Isaac - wounded, maimed and disabled in the service of his country, 1/2 pay of a Lt. in the Maryland Line. 1785: Chapt. 17

Hanspan, John Cadlep - of AA co., MD, an old soldier, 1/2 pay of a Pvt.. 1817:R23

Harmon, Lazarus - to receive 1/2 pay of what he would receive in Continental service, chargeable to the U.S. 1791:1

Harper, Elizabeth - , wid. of Samuel, 1/2 pay of a Pvt. 1831:47

Harper, William - 1/2 pay of a Pvt. 1812:54
    Harper, Bethula, of DO Co., wid. of William Harper, 1/2 pay of a Pvt. 1845:21

Harris, Arthur - an act for the relief of, late of the Continental Army. 1786: Chapt.19

Harris, Richard - soldier in the Maryland Line, never applied for his depreciation pay, he having lived outside the state, to receive 77 lbs, 6p, 1/2 penny, the amount due. 1797:Res.

Harris, Solomon - of DO co., MD, 1/2 pay of a Pvt. 1812:42

Harrison, Kinsey - of AA co. MD, 1/2 pay of a Pvt. 1816:12

Harrison, Robert H. - Pay representatives, Sarah Easton and Dorothy Storer, the sum equal to 1/2 pay for 3 years of an Aide-de-Camp to the Commander-in-Chief. 1839:28

Williams, Nancy - wid. of John Hartshorn, 1/2 pay of a Lt. 1835:17

Harvey, Zadoc - of DO co., MD, an "old Revolutionary Soldier", 1/2 pay of a Pvt. 1811:37

Hawman, Elizabeth - Pay to Philip and Frederick Hawman, legal heirs of, $10.00. bal of her pension due at time of her death. 1849:48

Hays, John - "Old Revolutionary Soldier", 1/2 pay of a Pvt. 1835:52

Hays, John H. - of StM co., MD, 1/2 pay of a Pvt. 1827:9
John H. Hays d. 29 Sept 1838, pay to Joseph F. Shaw for use of Theresa Hays, his widow bal. due at his death. 1838:6
Theresa Hays - of StM. co., MD, widow of John H. Hays, 1/2 pay of a Pvt. 1849:75

Haywood, Thomas - of StM co., MD, 1/2 pay of a Pvt. 1831:78

Hazelip, Richard - of WA co., MD, 1/2 pay of a Pvt. 1820:33

Head, John - 1/2 pay of a Pvt. 1818:58

Heaton, Elizabeth - of Berks co., PA, widow of James Heaton, 1/2 pay of a Pvt. 1826:41

Hempston, Wm. - of MT co., MD, an old Revolutionary Soldier, 1/2 pay of a Pvt. 1818:66
Pay bal. due at his death to son, Nathan T. Hempston of MT co., MD. 1833:51

Hewitt, James - 1/2 pay of a Pvt. 1818:55

Hill, John - 1/2 pay of a Pvt. 1812:39

Hill, George, - of AA co., MD, heir and representative of John Hill, who d. 5 Feb. 1828 pay balance due him. 1827:25

Hill, Richard - Soldier of the Revolution - pay to Lydia Brown and Ann Hill of StM co., legal representatives, warrant for 50 a. in AL co., MD. 1831:31

Hillman, William - 1/2 pay of a "soldier" for his "relief from indigence, misery...and old age." 1812:60
    Pay widow, Sally of SO co., Md, 1/2 pay of a Pvt. 1832:42
    Pay Constance D. Stanford for use of Nancy Stanford, Elizabeth Smith, and Biddy Hillman, heirs of Sally Hillman, wid. of William, decd. bal. $20.00. 1845:13

Holland, Jacob - late a Revolutionary soldier, now a commissioned officer, 1/2 pay of a Corp. of Dragoons. 1818:81

Holland, James - 1/2 pay of a Pvt. 1818:69

Holland, John - 1/2 pay of a Pvt. 1836:38

Holland, Joseph - 1/2 pay of a Pvt. 1818:69

Holland, Mary, widow of Edward Holland, 1/2 pay of a drummer, for services of her husband during the Revolutionary War. 1835:25

Hollydyoak, John - To widow, Ann of Annapolis, MD, 1/2 pay of a Pvt. 1826:43

Hood, Edward - of AA co., MD, 1/2 pay of a Pvt. 1821:58

Hood, James - of AA co., MD, 1/2 pay of an Asst. Commissary. 1817:33
    Hood, Kitty - widow of James, 1/2 pay of a Lt. 1831:90
    Pay to Isaiah Hood balance of pension due to Kitty Hood at the time of her death. 1846:10

Hook, Joseph - 1/2 pay of a Corp. 1815:9

Hooper, Abraham - of HA co., MD, an "old Revolutionary Soldier", 1/2 pay of a Pvt. 1816:31

Hoops, Adam - of Watervleit, Albany co., NY, 1/2 pay of a Capt. 1832:35

Hopkins, David - His merits ... established by letters from Gen. George Washington and his aides and Gens. Heath and Maylan; unable to earn a scanty subsistence for his wife and five children, 1/2 pay of a Capt. of Horse. 1805:Res.

Horner, Frances - widow of late Dr. Gustavus Horner, 1/2 pay of a Surgeon's Mate. 1833:35

Horney, Wm. - of TA co., MD, an "old Revolutionary Soldier" 1/2 pay of a "soldier" as relief from his indigence and misery which attend his decrepitude and old age. 1810:11

Hoskins, Mrs. - order for $20.00 for her support, her only son being in the army. CH co. Court, 1778

Hoskins, Randall - alias Randolph Hoskins of WA co., KY, 1/2 pay of a Pvt. 1828:41

House, Michael - of WA co., MD, 1/2 pay of a Pvt. 1821:56
    To Christiana House of WA co., MD, widow of Michael House, 1/2 pay of a Pvt. 1826:75

Howard, Benjamin - Warrant for 50 a. of "Soldier's Land" in AL co., MD. 1831:37

Howard, John - of Mason Co., KY, 1/2 pay of a Pvt. 1838:52

Howard, Col. John Eager - one of Maryland's most distinguished officers in the War of the Revolution...who d. this past year...portrait provided for the House of Delegates. 1827:23

Hudson, Elizabeth, of CA co., MD, widow of John Hudson, 1/2 pay
of a Pvt. 1827:54

Hughs, Mrs __ - wife of John Hughs for her support and her three
female children from the time of her husband's enlistment to
this day, $40.00 current money. CH co. Ct., Nov. 1782.

Hurdle, Lawrence - 1/2 pay of a Sgt. 1816:22

Hurst, Samuel - "an old soldier" of DO co., MD, 1/2 pay of a Pvt.
1817:15
    Stricken from the roll, having been found not in reduced
circumstances. 1819

Hutson, John - of CA co., MD, 1/2 pay of a Pvt. 1817:12 See
Elizabeth Hudson above.

Imeson, John - a soldier in the Revolutionary War, 15 lbs.
annually. 1803:6

Ireland, George - Register of the Land Office directed to issue
warrant to his legal rep. for 200 acres of vacant land westward of Ft. Cumberland in AL co., MD. 1828:55
    Requirement for location of land westward of Ft. Cumberland repealed. 1831:41
    Ireland, George - Officer in the Rev., pay legal rep.
$250.00 in lieu of 200 A of land in AL co., MD. 1838:31
    Ireland, Mary - of CT co., Md., wid. of George Ireland,
1/2 pay of a Lt. 1827:53

Isabell, Elizabeth - of Annapolis, 1/2 pay of a Sgt. 1821:36

Jackson, Ann - of Annapolis, 1/2 pay of a Sgt. 1821:57

Jacob, John J. - to receive sum of money in addition to that he
already receives under 1811:36, to make the amount he
receives equal to 1/2 pay of a 1st Lt. 1816:40

Jacob, John J. - Register of the Land Office to issue warrant to Jacob, late an officer in the Revolution, for 200 acres of land westward of Ft. Cumberland, in AL co., MD. 1829:27

> Jacob, John J. - A portion of Resolution 1830:27 which requires land granted be located westward of Ft. Cumberland, repealed. 1831:40

Jacob, John J. - a Revolutionary Soldier - to be paid $22.12 being the amount of composition money paid by him upon certain lands in AL co. but were found to be escheated and patented to Edward Norwood. 1830:27

Jacobs, William - of Hampshire co., VA, 1/2 pay of a Pvt. 1826:21

Jaquet, John D. - 1/2 pay of a Sgt. 1815:36

James, Leonard - of CE co., 1/2 pay of a Pvt. 1817:18

Jay, Martha, wid. of Alexander Lawson Smith, 1/2 pay of a Capt. 1835:40

Jeffries, Jacob - of QA co., 1/2 pay of a Pvt. 1816:52

Jenkins, Sarah - wid. of Philip Jenkins, 1/2 pay of a Pvt. 1836:20

Jenkins, Thomas, of DC, 1/2 pay of Pvt. 1829:6

Johnson, Archibald - of CH co., MD, 1/2 pay of a Sgt. 1812:46

Johnson, Rebecca - of QA co., MD, widow of Nicholas Johnson (Johnston), 1/2 pay of a Pvt. 1834:48

Johnston, William - of HA co., 1/2 pay of a Pvt. 1826:22

Jones, Aaron - of DO co., 1/2 pay of a Pvt. 1815:14

Jones, Cotter - of SO co., 1/2 pay of a Pvt. 1826:58

Jones, Lillias M. - of CH co., MD, dau. of Capt. Samuel Jones, officer in the MD Line, Register of Land Office to issue a warrant for 200 A. westward of Ft. Cumberland in AL co., MD. 1827:43

Jones, Nancy - of WO co., MD, 1/2 pay of a Pvt. 1833:40

Jones, Neale - 1/2 pay of a Pvt. 1812:58

Jones, Solomon - of DO co., Md, spent many of his younger years in military service; is now upwards of 73 yrs. and his wife nearly the same; both are infirm; petitions for support. Granted not in excess of $30.00 per yr., each. 1805:45

Jones, Thomas - of AA co., Md., 1/2 pay of a Pvt. 1833:63

Jones, William - formerly of PG co., now of VA, 1/2 pay of a Pvt. 1819:22

Jones, William - of CA co., MD, 1/2 pay of a Pvt. 1832:51

Kelly, Martha - of CR co., widow of William Kelly, soldier of the Revolution, 1/2 pay of a Capt. commencing 1 Jan. 1839. 1838:52

Kelly, Patrick - soldier in the German Regt., depreciation pay to be liquidated in the same manner as any other soldier. 1788:Res.

Kent, Isaac - of State of OH, 1/2 pay of a Pvt. in Maryland Line. 1819:28

Kershner, Mary Ann - of AL co., MD, 1/2 pay of a Pvt. [Husband's name not given]. 1826:35

Pay to Jacob Lantz, for use of Mrs. Mary C. Shryer, of AL co., MD, next and near friend of Mrs. Mary A. Kershner, deceased, balance due at her death. 1831:63

Kershner, Michael - of AL co., 1/2 pay of a Pvt. 1815:40

Kilty, Catharine - widow of late Capt. John Kilty, 1/2 pay of her late husband. 1821:8

Kindle, William - of WA co., 1/2 pay of a Pvt. 1817:13

King, George - 1/2 pay of a Pvt. 1818:67

King, Henry - 1/2 pay of a "Commissary". 1817:50

King, Margaret - widow of Levin King, late of SO co., MD, 1/2 pay of an Ensign. 1831:74
    Pay legal representative of Margaret King, balance due her on date of her death, 12 Sept. 1839. 1840:7. Repealed the next year (1841:7 session) and ordered amount of pension due her at time of her death be paid to the administrators.

King, Thomas - Pay $50.00 immediately and 1/2 pay of a Sgt; belonged to an Artillery co. of the City of Annapolis, was wounded in the Revolutionary War; lost his right hand while discharging a cannon; has a family dependent on him for support. 1808:3.

King, Thomas - Sgt. pensioned in 1809, now to be paid to wife, Mary King. 1811:2

Kline, Mary M. - of FK co., MD, widow of John Kline, 1/2 pay of a Pvt. 1833:65

Knight, Jacob - of OH, 1/2 pay of a Pvt. 1819:38

Koine (Coyn), Dominick - of HA co., MD, "an old infirm soldier", $40.00 annually during his life. 1803:2
  Pay to widow, Mary of HA co., MD, 1/2 pay of a Pvt. 1823:33

Lamb, Margaret - Widow of Richard White, 1/2 pay of a Pvt. 1834:11

Lambert, Christopher - of BA city, MD, 1/2 pay of a Pvt. 1837:47

Langford, Elijah - of SO co., MD, 1/2 pay of a Pvt. 1812:47

Lansdale, Cornelia - wid. of Maj. Thomas Lansdale, 1/2 pay of a Major. 1849:73

Lashley, George - of CE co., MD, 1/2 pay of a Pvt. 1826:64
  Pay to Granville S. Townsend $20.44 for benefit of Mary Sproul and Nancy Lashley, heirs of George Lashley, decd., bal. due Lashley at his death. 1835:107

Laurentz, Ann - of BA city, MD, wid. of Vandel Laurentz, a soldier of the Revolution, 1/2 pay of a Pvt. 1837:36

Law, William - 1/2 pay of a Pvt. 1816:13

Layman, William -1/2 pay of a Lt. 1816:34

Leake, (Leeke) of MT co., 1/2 pay of a Sgt. 1816:39
  Pay to James Brown of MT co., $10.00 due Henry Leake, late of MT co., a pensioner of the state. 1819:32

Leather, John - of FK co., MD, an old Revolutionary Soldier, 1/2 pay of a Sgt. 1816:27

Lee, Dudley - 1/2 pay of a "Soldier" as relief from the indigence and misery which attend his old age . 1811:24

Lee, Margaret - widow of Dudley Lee, 1/2 pay of a Pvt. 1837:44

Lee, Mary - widow of Parker Lee, Lt. in the 4th MD Regt. in the American Revolution, 1/2 pay of a Lt. 1849:62

Leonard, James - an "old soldier" of CE co., MD. 1/2 pay of a Pvt. 1817:18
    Register of Land Office to issue a warrant for 50 a. of land in AL co., MD to which he is entitled for services in the Revolution. 1825:98

Lewis, William - of WA co., MD, 1/2 pay of a Sgt. 1819:33

Lewis, William - of WA co., MD, in lieu of his present pension, 1/2 pay of a Capt. in Rev. and the war against the Indians. 1825:43
    To Mary Lewis, of WA co., MD, 1/2 pay of a Capt. [her late husband] Capt. William Lewis, Revolutionary Soldier. 1827:55

Lingan, Thomas - 1/2 pay of a Lt. 1822:48
    Lingan, Jannet - of MT co., MD, 1/2 pay of Capt. 1830:43

Lloyd, Thomas - of Philadelphia, PA, 1/2 pay of a Pvt. 1819:26
    Pay to Mary, widow of Thomas Lloyd, of PA, 1/2 pay of a Pvt. and the balance due her husband at his death. 1845:54

Lomax, John - 1/2 pay of a Pvt. 1818:74

Long, John - of HA co., MD, 1/2 pay of a Pvt. 1817:11

Long, William - of Missouri, 1/2 pay of a Pvt. 1839:54

Lorantz, Elizabeth, of BA city, widow of Ferdinand Lorantz, 1/2 pay of a Pvt. 1838:60

Lord, Andrew - of BA city, 1/2 pay of a Pvt. 1815:45
   To heirs of Andrew Lord of BA city, a warrant for 50 a. westward of Ft. Cumberland and if no heirs then to Amelia Lord, widow. of Andrew. 1827:47

Lord, Henry - of DO co., MD, 1/2 pay of a Pvt. 1819:35
   Pay bal. due - $12.44, 3 mos. 22 days - to Amelia Lord of DO co., MD, wid. of Henry Lord. 1838:7
   Amelia Lord - wid. of Henry Lord, 1/2 pay of a Pvt. to start 1 Jan. 1839. 1838:22

Lucas, Basil - "an old Revolutionary Soldier", 1/2 pay of a Sgt. 1815:63

Lucas, John - of AA co., MD, "an old Revolutionary Soldier" 1/2 pay of a Sgt. 1819:27
   Lucas, Rachel - Wid. of John Lucas of AA co., MD, 1/2 pay of a Pvt. 1831:73

Lynch, Hugh - 1/2 pay of a Pvt. in the MD Line. 1812:26

Lynch, Thomas - Revolutionary Soldier of StM co., MD, 1/2 pay of a Pvt. 1827:38
   Pay to James M. K. Hammett, administrator of, money due Lynch on 13 Nov. last [1831] the date of his death. 1832:50 CHECK

Lynn, John - wounded, maimed and disabled in the service of his country, 1/2 pay of a Lt. in Maryland Line. 1785:Chapt. 17
   Eleanor - wid.of John, 1/2 pay of a Lt. 1817:52
   Pay bal. due Eleanor, who d. 23 Apr. 1824, wid. of Col. John Lynn, to David Richardson, who intermarried with Elizabeth, one of the daughters of the deceased and to

Jane Lynn, another of her daughters, only heirs and representatives of the deceased. 1824:6

Lynn, Mary - wid. of David, 1/2 pay of a Capt. during her widowhood. 1835:43

Lynn, Valentine -soldier in the 3rd Maryland Regt., to receive interest on depreciation pay (1 Aug.1780 to 1 Jan. 1781). 1796:Res.
Soldier in the lst Maryland Regt, to receive depreciation pay of 56 lbs, 13 sh, 1p. 1796:Res.

McCann, Michael - of FK co., "an old soldier of the Revolution," 1/2 pay of a Pvt. 1817:31

McConnell, Samuel - of CE co., MD, 1/2 pay of a Sgt. 1812:57

McCracken, James - of HA co., MD, 1/2 pay of a Pvt.. 1825:60
McCracken, Mary - of HA co., Md., widow of James, 1/2 pay of a Pvt. 1843:18

M'Gee, Charles - 1/2 pay of a Pvt. 1815:39

McGee, William - 1/2 pay of a Pvt. 1815 :12 *See Magee.

McKinsey, Moses - of AL co., MD, 1/2 pay of a Drummer. 1815:23
McKinsey, Sarah, - of AL Co., MD, widow of Moses, 1/2 pay of a Pvt. 1826:44

McLean, Arthur - of BA co., MD, Revolutionary Soldier, 1/2 pay of Sgt. 1828:8

McNemara, Darby - An old infirm and disabled soldier, pay annual sum of $57.00 in lieu of $399.00, principal and interest due on three State Certificates as depreciation of his pay; first payment to be made 10 Dec. 1798:Res.

Pay to Darby McNemara, a poor and disabled soldier of the lst MD Regt. 25 lbs, 6 sh. 11 d. with interest from 1 Aug. 1780 for a depreciation certificate issued to him and [now] lost. 1799:Res.

Pay 15 lbs. annually to Darby McNemara, a soldier in the Revolutionary war by which he as been rendered entirely unable to obtain a subsistence. 1802:Res.

McPherson, Mark - 1/2 pay of a Lt. 1815:10
Pay to Christian Keener, attorney for Walter McPherson, executor of Mark McPherson, amount due at time of his death. 1847:23

McQuinny, Thomas - 1/2 pay of a Pvt. 1818:76

Magee, William - Pay bal. due to widow, Sarah of StM. co., MD 1829:36

Magruder, Nathaniel B. - 1/2 pay of a Lt. 1815:20

Mahoney, Clement - an old Revolutionary Soldier, 1/2 pay of a Pvt. 1815:5

Mahooney, Edward - 1/2 pay of a Pvt. 1811:60

Mantz, Catharine - widow of Peter Mantz, 1/2 pay of a Major. 1845:23

Markland, Edward - of City of BA, 1/2 pay of a Lt. in Navy, 1823:3
Markland, Alice - widow of Edward, 1/2 pay of a Lt. in Navy. 1838:12

Marr, William - To his wid., Arra Marr, 1/2 pay of a Pvt. the rest of her life. 1835:18

Marshall, Benjamin - warrant for 50 a. of unappropriated land in AL co., MD as a donation granted to Revolutionary soldiers in the Maryland Line. 1825:105

Marshall, John - of CE co., MD 1/2 pay of a Pvt. 1832:80

Martin, Dr. Ennals - of TA co., Md, 1/2 pay of a Surgeon's Mate. 1832:2
    Martin, Sarah - widow of Dr. Ennals Martin of TA co., MD, 1/2 pay of a Surgeons Mate. 1834:9

Martin, Henry - of FK co., MD, Revolutionary soldier, 1/2 pay of Pvt. 1827:12

Martin, Margaret - of Westmoreland co., PA, widow of Jacob Martin, a Revolutionary Soldier with the MD troops, 1/2 pay of a Pvt. 1845:47

Maxwell, James of CE co., MD, "a meritorious soldier," 1/2 pay of a Corp., in his indigent situation , now advanced in life. 1811:14

May, Isaac - native of MD, Lt. in Navy in Rev. [in battle] *Hornet* vs the British *Peacock*; *Hornet* vs. the British *Penguin*; received a medal from the U.S. -to receive a sword. 1827:61

Mayhew, Jonathan - 1/2 pay of a Pvt. 1818:77
    Eleanor L. - widow of Jonathan Mayhew of WA co., MD, 1/2 pay of a Pvt. 1833:32
    Pay to Adam Houk, s/l, of the late Eleanor L. Mayhew, $8.00, for 2 mos, 12 days pension due her at date of her death, on 12 Dec.1837. 1837:2

Meddagh, Frederick - of FK co., MD, a superannuated soldier of the late American Army, to be granted a peddlar's license by the various county courts with out paying for such. 1801:15

Medlar, Bostian - 1/2 pay of a Drum Maj. 1815:11

Merrick, William - of DO co., MD, 1/2 pay of a Corp. 1820:44

Merryman, Elizabeth - widow of Luke Merryman, Revolutionary Soldier, 1/2 pay of a Pvt. 1835:51

Middleton, Gilbert - of BA city, 1/2 pay of a Capt. 1822:11
    Middleton, Sarah - of BA city, MD, widow of Capt. Middleton. 1/2 pay of a Capt. 1821:22

Miles, Jane - widow of Joshua Miles, an officer in the Revolution, 1/2 pay of a Capt. 1835:93. Rescinded and re-written 1835:117

Miller, George - of BA city, 1/2 pay of a Pvt. 1826:36

Mills, Zachariah - of AA co., MD, and old Revolutionary soldier, 1/2 pay of a Pvt. 1819:43

Minitree, Paul - of CH co., MD, an old Revolutionary soldier. 1/2 pay of a Pvt. 1818:54

Mitchell, Charles - Pvt. in the Flying Camp, not Continental, stricken from the Roll. Jan. 1820, p. 547

Montle (or Mondle), George, now of PA, late soldier in the MD Line 1/2 pay of a "soldier" (no rank given). 1817:27

Moore, John - late a soldier in the extra Maryland regt., the sum of $22.00. 1798:Res.

Moore, Sarah - resident of BA city, widow of Nicholas R[uxton] Moore, 1/2 pay of a Lt. 1833:36

Moore, Sarah, of BA city, widow of Nicholas R.- 1/2 pay of a Capt. of Cavalry, in lieu of 1/2 pay of a Lt, heretofore granted. 1839:6

Moore, Rueben - of DO co., MD, 1/2 pay of a Pvt. 1818:62
    Pay Mary of DO co., MD, widow of Rueben Moore, 1/2 pay of a Pvt. 1826:48

Moore, William - of SO co., MD, 1/2 pay of a Pvt.. 1832:65
    Pay bal. due William Moore to his son, Samuel T. Moore, of SO co. 1834:8

Morris, John - of StM co., MD, late a soldier in the 3rd MD Regt, disabled from wounds received at the battle of Cowpens, and is incapable of getting a livelihood, 1/2 pay of that he received in the service [rank not stated]; to be billed to the U.S. 1791:Res.

Morris, Jonathan - of Washington co., PA, 1/2 pay of a Capt. 1829:13

Mudd, Mrs. Barbara - of DC, 1/2 pay of a Sgt. 1833:13

Mudd, Bennett - of CH co., MD, 1/2 pay of a Sgt. 1818:59
    Pay to Ann Mudd, $24.17, the amount of pension due her husband at his death and was forfeited by resolution of 1823:26. 1834:5
    Ann Mudd - widow of Bennett Mudd, 1/2 pay of a Sgt. 1835:118

Muir, Thomas - 1/2 pay of a Pvt. 1831:25
    Muir, Thomas - of SO co., MD. Pay bal. due to Levin Ballard of Jarvis, $9.66 for use of heirs. 1838:9

Murdock, Benjamin - 1/2 pay of a Lt. in the MD Line. 1817:28

Murdock, Patrick - to receive $40.00 as full compensation for Lot no. 3876, westward of Ft. Cumberland, in AL co., which was sold by the state. 1805:Res.
    Clagett, Jane - wid. of William Murdock - 1/2 pay of a Lt. 1833:34

Nagle, Richard - of Cambria co., PA, 1/2 pay of a Pvt. 1827:16

Neale, Eleanor - widow of Capt. Henry Neale, 1/2 pay of a Capt. 1836:35

Neale, James - to receive 15 lbs. annually as support to him in his infirm situation and for services in the late Revolutionary War, which has rendered him entirely unable to obtain a subsistence. 1803:Res.

Needham, William A. - [of MT co., MD], 1/2 pay of a Sgt. having been wounded by a musket ball which passed through his body, and rendered him incapable of gaining a subsistence; to be charged to the U.S. 1791:Res.

Nelson, Eliza - widow of Roger Nelson of FK co., MD, 1/2 pay from 1 July 1815, to which her husband would have been entitled as a Lt. of Cavalry. 1833:37
    Nelson, Eliza - widow of Roger Nelson, Revolutionary officer, of FK co., MD, 1/2 pay of a Lt. from 1 July 1815 until she was placed on the pension roll under act of 1779. 1838:39

Newman, John - 1/2 pay of a Sgt. 1816:11
    Pay bal. due to William Ridgely, Esq. 1830:5

Newton, John - 1/2 pay of a Pvt. 1817:24

Niblet, John - of WO co., MD, an old Revolutionary soldier, 1/2 pay of a Pvt. 1816:18

Nowell, James and Jonathan Tutwiller - each 1/2 pay of a Pvt. 1812:35

O'Bryan, Dennis - of Morgan co., VA [now WV], an old Revolutionary soldier, 1/2 pay of a Pvt. 1829:32

O'Connor, Michael - of HA co., MD, 1/2 pay of a Matross. 1812:61

O'Hara, Susan - widow of John O'Hara, 1/2 pay of a Pvt. 1839:14

Onion, Juliet - wid. of William Pendergast, 1/2 pay of a Lt. 1834::41

Orem, Spedden - of TA co., MD, 1/2 pay of a Pvt. 1824:23

Orme, Moses - of AA co., MD, 1/2 pay of a Pvt. 1832:49

Orndorff, Christian - 1/2 pay of a Capt. 1818:82

Ott, Adam - of WA co., MD, 1/2 pay of a Lt. 1821:46
    Pay to Juliana Ott - of WA co., MD, widow of Adam Ott, arrears due him as pensioner at his death. 1828:25
    Pay to Juliana Ott, of WA co., MD, widow of Adam Ott, Revolutionary Soldier, 1/2 pay of a Lt. 1827:44

Painter, Mary - of WA co., MD, widow of Melchoir Painter, 1/2 pay of a Pvt. 1838:62

Parran, Thomas - to heirs of, warrant and patent to 200 a of land westward of Ft. Cumberland. (Rank not stated). 1827:40

Parran, Dr. Thomas - Surgeon in the Revolution - pay to Mrs. Jane, his widow, 1/2 a Surgeon's pay. 1827:52
    Parran, Jane - decd. Pay balance of pension due her to her legal representative. 1829:4

Parrish, Edward - of BA co., MD, 1/2 pay of a Sgt. 1826:32
   Pay to James Nelson $6.00 for use of Clemency Parrish, wid. of Edward Parrish decd., late of BA co., MD, Revolutionary Soldier, amount due at his death. 1835:49
   Pay to Clemency Parrish, 1/2 pay of a Sgt. 1855:33

Parrot, Christopher - 1/2 pay of a Sgt. 1816:29

Patten, Coleman - of BA co., now upwards of 65 yrs.; served six yrs. in the Revolutionary War, wounded in the thigh, which occasions him to halt in that member - petitions the Assembly for support. Granted. 1803:78

Paul, Catharine - widow of Thomas, 1/2 pay of a Sgt. 1839:22

Peacock, Neal - 1/2 pay of a Pvt. 1812:48

Pearce, George - of Warren co., KY, 1/2 pay of a Pvt. 1832:37

Pegegram, William - of AA co., an old Revolutionary soldier, 1/2 pay of a common soldier. 1811:23

Penefield, Hester - widow of Thomas, 1/2 pay of a Pvt. 1834:76

Penn, John - of CH co., MD, 1/2 pay of a Pvt. 1820:46

Philips, Stephen - of CA co., MD, "a coloured man," 1/2 pay of a Pvt. 1820:37
   Pay to Jacob Charles, $13.33, money he advanced Stephen Philips. 1843:21

Pindell, Nicholas - Pay bal. due at death to Gassaway Pindell, admns. 1830:32

Pindell, Dr. Richard - of KY, full pay as Surgeon. 1816:58

Plane, Jacob - Pay to widow, Catherine Plane of AA co., MD, 1/2 pay of a Pvt. 1830:56

Poe, Elizabeth - widow of BA city, 1/2 pay of a Capt. in the Maryland Line. 1821:23

Popham, Benjamin - of AA co., MD. 1/2 pay of a Pvt. 1826:63

Porter, Nathan - of TA co., MD, 1/2 pay of a Pvt. 1824:27

Powers, Jesse - of StM co., MD, 1/2 pay of a Pvt. 1815:13
    Powers, Milly - widow of Jesse, 1/2 pay of a Pvt. 1835:41
    Pay to Henry Fowler, for use of Clement Thompson, legal rep. of Milly Powers, balance due her at time of her death. 1844:6

Price, George - of TA co., MD, 1/2 pay of a Pvt. 1826:31
    Pay to representative balance of pension due him at death. 1828:61

Price, Stephen R. - of Mifflin Twsp, Franklin co., OH, 1/2 pay of Quartermaster Sgt. 1829:47

Proctor, Richard - 1/2 pay of a Pvt. in the MD Line. as provision "in his indigent situation and advanced life." 1811:40

Pruitt, Walter - of WO co., MD, 1/2 pay of a Pvt. 1826:46

Queen, Marsham - of CH co., MD, 1/2 pay of a Pvt. 1831:106

Quinny, Thomas M. - 1/2 pay of a Pvt. 1818:76

Rasin, William B. - of KT co., Md, 1/2 pay of a Lt. 1804:Res.

Rawlings, Ann - wid. of Samuel Rawlings, late of WA co., MD, decd., 1/2 pay of a Pvt. 1821:55

Rawlings, Solomon - 1/2 pay of a Pvt. 1818:79

Ray, Joseph - an old soldier of MT co., MD, 1/2 pay of a Pvt. 1817:21

Reading, Henry - 1/2 pay of a Pvt. in the MD Line. 1811:9

Reid, John - of AL co., MD, $125.00 quarterly. [Rank not given] 1812:40

Reily, William - of the DC, 1/2 pay of a Capt. in MD Line. 1816:30
    Reily, Barbara - of the DC, wid. of Major William Reily, 1/2 pay of a Capt. 1832:40

Reynolds, Ruth - widow of James Reynolds, 1/2 pay of a Pvt. 1834:50

Reynolds, Tobias - of AA Co., MD, an "old soldier," 1/2 pay of a Pvt. 1817:26

Richards, Mary - of BA city, widow of Paul Richards, 1/2 pay of a Pvt. 1822:61
    To heirs and representatives of Mary, widow of Paul Richards, soldier in the Revolution, the sum due her at her death. 1827:50

Richardson, Charles - 1/2 pay of a Pvt., provision to him in his indigent situation and advanced life. 1812:52
    Richardson, Nancy - widow of Charles Richardson, 1/2 pay of a Pvt. 1820:49 or 1819?
    Pay Lydia Ackworth, dau. of Nancy Richardson, amount of pension due said Nancy at her death. 1845:49

Richardson, Daniel - 1/2 pay of a Pvt. 1811:25

Rigby, William - of Fairfield co., OH, 1/2 pay of a Quartermaster Sgt. 1819:29

Risdon, (als. Riston), Zadock - of PG co., Md, 1/2 pay of a Pvt. 1829:48
    Risdon (als. Riston), Zadock - late of PG co., MD - pay bal. due at death to Benjamin Riston and Cassandra Ann King, only children of Zadock. 1838:42

Robbins, John - of MT co., MD, "an old soldier", 1/2 pay of a Pvt. 1817:16

Robosson, Rebecca - of BA city, widow of Charles Robosson, half pay of a 1st Lt. 1838:21

Roberts, William - of AL co., MD, 1/2 pay of a Pvt. 1815:21
    Roberts, Jane - of AL co., MD, wid. of William, 1/2 pay of a Pvt. 1833:33
    Roberts, Jane - wid. of William, pay bal. due $1.11. 1834:24
    Pay amt. due ($9.89) to Mary Roberts of AL co., MD for 2 mos., 29 days pension due Jane Roberts of AL co. MD at the time of her death. 1838:40

Roberts, Zachariah - Pay to Peter Lovering of BA city, MD, 1/2 pay of a Corp. for support of Roberts. 1822:55

Robertson, Eleanor - former wid. of Charles Willin, 1/2 pay of a Seaman and Pvt. 1838:23

Robinson, Standly - of BA city, 1/2 pay of a Pvt. on board the *Dolphin* during the Revolutionary War. 1823:37

Roby, John - 1/2 pay of a Pvt. 1815:6

Rolle, Robert, of TA co., MD, Revolutionary soldier, 1/2 pay of a Lt. 1828:65

Rouark, James - Pay to Julia, widow of James Rouark, soldier of the Revolution, 1/2 pay of a Pvt. during her widowhood. 1835:42

Rowse, Thomas - 1/2 pay of a Lt. in the MD Line. 1811:13

Ruark, Barbara - wid. of James, 1/2 pay of a Pvt. 1847:26
    Pay to William Wells, of AA co., amount of pension due Mrs. Barbara Ruark. 1837:19

Rutledge, Joshua - of HA co., MD in the MD Line, 1/2 pay of a Lt. 1812:41
    Resolution granting Joshua Rutledge a pension is revoked due to the fact that he is "wealthy" and the intention of the legislature is to assist such as are in need and not those who are living in affluence. 1821:61
    Pay to Elizabeth Brooks, wid. of Joshua Rutledge, 1/2 pay of a Lt. 1839:13

Sansbury, Sarah - of BA city, wid. of John Sansbury, 1/2 pay of a Pvt. Marine. 1839:8

Sappington, Cassandra - of HA co., MD, widow of Dr. Richard Sappington, 1/2 pay of a Surgeon. 1843:34

Schrach, Andrew - of BA city, MD, Rev. Sold. 1/2 pay of a Pvt. 1828:51

Scott, Samuel - 1/2 pay of a Pvt. 1816:63
    Pay bal. due at time of death to Benjamin L. Gantt for use of Mrs. Elizabeth Scott, widow of Samuel Scott of PG co., MD, $14.44. 1833:23

Elizabeth Scott, wid, of Samuel Scott, of PG co., 1/2 pay of a Pvt. 1833:42

Pay to order of William Scott, legal rep. of Elizabeth Scott, of PG co., decd., bal. of pension due her at her death. 1847:11

Scrivner, Sarah - of BA city, former widow of William Whitaker, 1/2 pay of a Pvt. 1838:24

Seaburn, John - 1/2 pay of a Pvt. 1811:12

Sears, Mary - of HA co., MD, wid. of John Sears, 1/2 pay of Lt. 1827:4

Second, George - pay $54.00 per anum. 1803:3. [The Index states his rank as Corp.]

Semmes, James - of CH co., MD, 1/2 pay of a 2nd Lt. 1812:59

Sewall, Charles - of CH Co., MD, 1/2 pay of a lst Lt., 1819:42

Sewell, Clement - of the DC, 1/2 pay of an Ensign. 1822:62

Sewell, James - an old Revolutionary soldier, 1/2 pay of a Pvt. 1817:34

Sewell, Rebecca - wid. of William, 1/2 pay of a Pvt. 1831:16

Sewell, William - of TA co., MD, 1/2 pay of a Pvt.. 1821:41

Sewell, William - of Annapolis, MD, 1/2 pay of a Pvt. 1811:11

Shane, Henry - pay bal. due to son, Henry W. Shane. 1830:17

Shean, Henry - of BA co., MD 1/2 pay of a Pvt. 1827:46

Sheets, Hannah - of FK co., MD, wid. of Jacob, 1/2 pay of a Pvt, 1827:3

Sherburn, Mary - to be paid depreciation pay due Charles Sherburn, for 12 mos. pay as a soldier in the lst Maryland Regt. 1796:Res.

Shircliff, Melinda - wid. of William, 1/2 pay of a Lt. 1837:55
    Pay balance due ($36.45) at her death, 22 Mar. 1840, to her son Leonard Shircliff, Esq. of AL co. 1840:21

Shirley, Susanna, widow of Bennett Shirley, 1/2 pay of a Pvt. 1836:12

Shoebrook, Edward - Pvt., pay to Joseph Boon of CA co., MD, for support of. 1822:70

Shotts, John - of FK co., MD, an old soldier, 1/2 pay of a Pvt. 1817:25

Shryack, John - 1/2 pay of a Pvt. 1834:60

Simmons, Aaron - 1/2 pay of a Pvt. 1818:72

Simmons, Sarah - of CH Co., MD, widow, 1/2 pay of a Pvt. 1833:31

Simpson, Lawrence - of CH co., MD, an old Revolutionary soldier, 1/2 pay of a Pvt. 1816:23
    Pay Peter W. Crain for use of wid. of Lawrence Simpson, bal. due at his death. 1842:24

Simpson, Rezin - 1/2 pay of a Pvt. 1812:37
    1/2 pay of a Sgt. of Dragoons in lieu of the sum allowed previously. 1815:52

Pay to Robert Swan bal. due Rezin Simpson at his death for the use of Mary Simpson, widow of Rezin Simpson, pensioner. 1829:29

Pay William Shaw for the use of Mary Simpson of AL co., MD, for services of her late husband, Rezin Simpson 1/2 pay of a Sgt. 1830:60

Simpson, Thomas - 1/2 pay of a Corp. 1812:62

Sizler, Philip - of BA city, Revolutionary soldier, 1/2 pay of a Sgt. in the Artillery. 1828:31

Smith, Alexander Lawson - Pay Martha Jay, his wid. 1/2 pay of a Capt. 1835:40

Smith, Aquilla - of KY, 1/2 pay of a Pvt. 1833-49

Smith, Benjamin - of KY, 1/2 pay of a Pvt. 1830:16

Smith, Charles - of TA co., MD, 1/2 pay of a Pvt. 1834:54

Smith, Charles - 1/2 pay of a Pvt. 1815:24

Smith, Mary - of the DC, wid. of Capt. Charles Smith, 1/2 pay of a Capt. 1833:54

Smith, Elijah - of BA city, an old soldier, 1/2 pay of a Pvt. 1817:32.

Pay bal. of pension due to Mrs. Priscilla Smith, widow of Elijah Smith, of BA city. 1825:113

Pay Priscilla Smith, widow of Elijah Smith, 1/2 pay of a Pvt. 1838:57

Smith, Ephriam - of BA city, 1/2 pay of a Pvt. 1842:8

Smith, John - of AA co. MD 1/2 pay of a Pvt. 1818:75

Smith, John - of AA co., 1/2 pay of a Pvt. 1824:50

Smith, John - of CH co., MD 1/2 pay of a Pvt. 1818:60

Smith, John - of PG co., MD 1/2 pay of a Corp. 1822:56
    Pay to Richard L. Jenkins of PG Co., MD, $6.97, amt. due John Smith at his death. 1842:3

Smith, Joseph - 1/2 pay of a Capt. in the MD Line. 1815:16

Smith, Nathaniel - To widow, Sarah Smith of BA city, 1/2 pay of a Capt. 1822:69
    To Sarah Smith, of BA city, widow of Nathaniel Smith, 1/2 pay of a Maj. in lieu of the 1/2 pay of a Capt. she now receives. 1826:45

Smith, Sarah - of AA co., MD, widow of John, 1/2 pay of a Pvt. 1831:119

Smith, Thomas - of Ohio, Revolutionary soldier, 1/2 pay of a Pvt. 1828:35

Smyth, Anna M. - widow of Thomas Smyth - 1/2 pay of a Lt.
    Smyth, Anna Maria - 1/2 pay of Maj. (late hus. Thomas Smyth) in lieu of pension by resolution, 1830:33, provided she relinquish claims for arrears. 1835:81

Somervell, Capt. James - Pay to James Somervell [Jr.], of PG co., son and one of the heirs, sum due to James, Sr. on the pension list at time of his death. 1827:41 (See below)

Somerville, James - 1/2 pay of a Capt. in the MD Line, maimed wounded and disabled. 1785: Chapt. 17

Spaulding, Aaron - 1/2 pay of a Sgt. 1815:28

Spaulding, Daniel - of BA, 1/2 pay of a Pvt. 1825:85
   Pay to Samuel Spaulding of BA, $19.06, balance due late Daniel Spaulding, provided Samuel is the only heir of Daniel. 1847:72

Spaulding, Henry - 1/2 pay of a Pvt., provision for him in his "indigent situation and advanced life." 1811:16

Spedden, Edward - of BA city, an old Revolutionary soldier, 1/2 pay of a 2nd. Lt.. 1819:48
   Spedden, Ann, - of BA city, MD, widow of Edward Spedden, 1/2 pay of a 2nd Lt. 1822:68

Spires, Richard - of Brown co., OH, 1/2 pay of a Pvt. 1828:42

Stanton, John - 1/2 pay of a Pvt. 1828:32

Staples, John - 1/2 pay of a Pvt. 1819:20
   Pay to Margaret Staples, widow of John Staples, 1/2 pay of a Sgt. 1844:37

Stephens, Levi - of SO co., 1/2 pay of a Pvt. 1815:38
   Pay to Polly, widow of Levi Stephens, 1/2 pay of a Pvt. 1834:27

Steuart, Elizabeth - of QA Co., MD 1/2 pay of a Capt. 1843:23
   Pay to Woolman I. Gibson, for the use of representatives of Elizabeth Stuart [sic], deceased, $33.33, the amount due per resolution 1843:23, to Feb. 21, 1849, the day of her death. 1849:71

Stevens, Benjamin - of SO Co., MD, an old soldier, 1/2 pay of a Pvt. 1816:16

Stevens, Levi - Pay to William W. Stevens and David Stevens, executors of Levi Stevens, $28.33, 8 mos., 15 days pension due at the time of his death. 1835:39 (See Levi Stephens above)

Stone, John - Pay to Dr. N. P. Cousin for use of the surviving child of John Stone the sum of 1/2 pay of a Col.; John Stone served in MD Line 1779-1782, 2 yrs. 11 mos, under Act of 1778, Chapt. 14, etc. 1838:38

Storer, Dorothy - widow, of the DC, 1/2 pay of a Capt.. 1826:33

Strap, Jacob - served 3 yrs. in the 1st Maryland Regt. and afterward was captured as sea by the British and was carried to Portsmouth in Great Britain where he was imprisoned until the restoration of peace. Being destitute, he could not return until Dec. 1787. He is to receive depreciation pay due him. 1788:Res.

Strider, Philip - late of Bedford co., PA who d. Jan. 16, 1840 - pay to M. C. Sprigg, legal representative of...$12.93, balance due him at death. 1840:13
    Sprigg, M. C. - legal representative of Philip Strider, a pensioner of the state of MD, late of Bedford Co., PA who d. 6 Jan. 1841, to be paid $12.93 due Strider from 10 Sept. 1840 until his death. 1841:13

Studer, Philip - 1/2 pay of a Pvt. 1815:24

Summers, Solomon - of QA co., MD, 1/2 pay of a Drummer. 1816:25

Swan, Leonard - "An old soldier," 1/2 pay of a Pvt. 1817:14

Tannehill, Mrs. Agnes M. - widow, of AL Co. PA, 1/2 pay of a Capt. 1825:70

Tasker, Richard - of AL co., MD, 1/2 pay of a Pvt. 1819:34

Taylor, John - of AA co., MD, 1/2 pay of a Pvt. 1833:53
    Taylor, Sega - of AA co., MD, amount due her husband, John Taylor, on the pension list of the state at time of his death. 1835:58

Taylor, Richard - 1/2 pay of a Pvt. 1815:30

Taylor, Sydney - widow of John Taylor, Revolutionary Soldier, 1/2 pay of a Pvt. 1835:82

Thomas, John Jarman - Revolutionary Soldier, 1/2 pay of Pvt. 1835:50

Thomas, Joseph - pay 1/2 pay of a Pvt. to his trustee, Frisby Henderson, Esq. of CE co., MD for his use. 1821:37

Thompson, Barnard - of WA co., KY, 1/2 pay of a Pvt. 1832:38

Thompson, Charles - of StM. co., MD, 1/2 pay of a Pvt. 1816:17

Thompson, Jesse - 1/2 pay of a Sgt. in the MD Line. 1812:25

Thompson, John - of KT co., MD, 1/2 pay of a Pvt. 1812:28

Thompson, Thomas - of DO co., MD, 1/2 pay of a Pvt. 1816:19
    Pay to, Mary Thompson, widow of Thomas Thompson, late of DO Co., 1/2 pay of a Pvt. 1819:47

TIllard, Sarah, wid. of Lt. Col. Tillard, 1/2 pay of a Capt. 1819:10. Pay to Otho Thomas Tillard of FK co., for the benefit of the heirs of Sarah Tillard, $57.33 due at the time of her death. 1834:58

Tillotson, Dr. Thomas - Surgeon of Rhinebeck Co., NY [Ed. note: there is no such co. in NY but there is a village of that name in Dutchess Co., NY], 1/2 pay of a Surgeon. 1829:42

Tillotson, Dr. Thomas - of NY, warrant for 200 a. in AL co., MD. 1831:111

Toomey, John - of QA co., MD, 1/2 pay of a Corp. 1819:29

Townsend, Allen - 1/2 pay of a Pvt. 1816:24

Townsend, Thomas - of TA co., MD, 1/2 pay of a Pvt. 1824:22

Truck, John - of FK co., MD, 1/2 pay of a Sgt. 1825:61

Truck, John - of FK co., MD, 50 a. of land in AL co., MD 1825:261

Trueman, John -1/2 pay of a Lt. in the MD Line, "Maimed, wounded and disabled." 1785: Chapt. 17

Trux, Elizabeth - of FK Co., MD, widow of John Trux, a soldier of the Revolutionary War, 1/2 pay of a Sgt. 1831:71

Turner, Thomas - of MT Co., MD, 1/2 pay of a Pvt. 1818:53

Tutwiller, Jonathan, 1/2 pay of a Pvt. 1812:35; also 1/2 pay of a Sgt. instead of a Pvt. as listed. 1815:60

Tydings, Kealy - 1/2 pay of a Sgt. 1811:22

Uncles, Benjamin - of AA co., MD, 1/2 pay of a Pvt. 1821:45
    To Rebecca, wid. of Benjamin Uncles, 1/2 pay of a Pvt. 1837:4
    Pay to Mrs. Sarah Earlougher, $6.67 balance due to Rebecca Uncles, deceased, at the time of her death. 1846:53

Vane, Lucretia - of DO Co., widow of John Vane, 1/2 pay of a Pvt. MD. 1826:57

Lucretia Vane d. 28 Sept. 1835. Balance of her pension, $9.77, to be paid to James Vane, one of her legal representatives. 1836:8 See 1825:18 CHCECK?????

Valdenar, Frances - executor of William Layman, late of MT Co., deceased, to be paid the amount due Layman at his death, 12 Feb. 1842. 1841:26

Varlow, Stephen - of CE co., MD, 1/2 pay of a Pvt. 1819:36

Vaughn, William - for meritorious service, 1/2 pay of a Pvt. 1812:55

Walker, John - of FK co., MD, 1/2 pay of a Corp. 1820:31
    Pay to Mary Walker, widow of John Walker, soldier of the Revolution, 1/2 pay of a Corp. 1847:35

Wall, William - an old soldier of DO co., MD, 1/2 pay of a Pvt. 1818:63
    Pay to Keturah (Kitturah) Wall, widow of William Wall, $10.78 being 3 mos. 7 days pension due her husband at his death. 1836:27
    Kitturah Wall, widow of William Wall, 1/2 pay of a Pvt. 1836:42

Walley, Zedikiah - commanded a galley of this State and was killed in combat in 1782 leaving one son, Thomas, who was then naturalized by act of the assembly and it was directed that he be educated at the expense of the State. Zedikiah, by his will (1779) devised to son Thomas and dau., Mary who has since died without issue. Your petitioner, Mary Walley, came from Ireland with her son, Thomas, who will come of age 28 Oct. 1796. If Thomas should die before coming of age, without issue, the estate will become the property of Zedikaiah Walley Grier.... 1784:36

Walls, Martha, of PG co., MD, 1/2 pay of a Pvt. 1839:51

Waltman, Michael - of FK co., MD, 1/2 pay of a Pvt. 1824:24
    To Mary Waltman of FK co., MD, wid. of Michael Waltman, 1/2 pay of a Pvt. 1839:33

Ware, Francis - Lt. Col. in the Revolution, who heretofore commanded troops of this state became reduced to extreme indigence...to receive 1/2 pay of a Lt. Col. 1800:7

Warring, Ann - wid. of Basil Warring, 1/2 pay of a Lt. 1833:43

Waters, Jonathan - 1/2 pay of a Pvt. 1818:52

Waters, Margaret - wid. of Dr. Wilson Waters, 1/2 pay of a Surgeons Mate. 1835:59

Waters, Richard - 1/2 pay of a Capt. in the MD Line. 1815:19

Waters, Richard - of BA city 1/2 pay of a Capt.. 1826:62
    Elizabeth J. Waters. widow of Richard Waters, 1/2 pay of a Capt. 1830:13

Watkins, Gassaway - 1/2 pay of a Capt. in lieu of sum already allowed him by Resolution in 1811. 1815:64

Watkins, Leonard - 1/2 pay of a Sgt. in MD Line. 1812:50
    Watkins, Mary - of MT co., widow of Leonard, of MT co., MD, 1/2 pay of a Sgt. 1838:37

Wats, James - of DO co., MD, 1/2 pay of a Pvt. 1832:10

Watson, Sarah Ann - widow of Lt. Col. William H. Watson, 1/2 pay equal to that proper of her late husband of the Infantry of the U.S. not to exceed $30.00 per month. 1849:63

Wells, Martha - of PG Co., MD, widow, 1/2 pay of a Pvt. 1839:51

West, Benjamin - of BA city, 1/2 pay of a Pvt. 1825:103

Wheatley, Rhoda - of DO co., MD, widow of William Wheatley, 1/2 pay of a Pvt. 1831-105
    Pay balance due on pension (2 mos. 5 days) to Esther Willis, Admnx. of Rhoda Wheatley who d. 5 June 1839. 1839:10

Wheeler, Mary - widow of Nathaniel Wheeler, 1/2 pay of a Pvt. 1831:19

White, James - of MT co., MD, 1/2 pay of a Pvt. 1822:60
    Pay to Henry Harding, bal. due the late James White, for the use of Priscilla White, his widow, the balance of his pension. 1829:19

White, Samuel B. - of MT co., MD, 1/2 pay of a Pvt. 1825:86
    Pay to Sarah, wid. of Samuel B. White of MT co., MD, 1/2 pay of a Pvt. 1831:70

White, Thomas - of BA co., MD, 1/2 pay of a Pvt. 1827:10

Wiery, Elizabeth, widow of Michael, of York co., PA, 1/2 pay of a Pvt. 1840:8

Wilkerson, Young - of AA Co., MD, 1/2 pay of a Lt. 1810:12

Wilkinson, James - 1/2 pay of a Col. of Dragoons. 1815:47

Williams, Charles - 1/2 pay of a Pvt. in MD line. 1812:27

Williams, Harriet - of Georgetown, DC, widow of Elisha, 1/2 pay of a Capt. 1832:34

Williams, John - of StM co., MD, 1/2 pay of a Corp. 1815:18

Williams, John - of BA city, MD, Revolutionary soldier, 1/2 pay of a Pvt. 1827:8

Williams, Joseph - of AA co., MD, warrant for 50 A. in AL co., MD. 1832:67

Williams, Joseph - of Annapolis, MD, 1/2 pay of a Pvt. 1823:32

Williams, Osborn - 1/2 pay of a Lt. 1818:65

Willins, Evans - Pay to widow, Mary Easom, of DO co., MD, 1/2 pay of a Pvt. 1831:44

Willin, Levin, Sr. - of SO co., MD, 1/2 pay of a Pvt. 1832:12

Willis, Andrew - of WA co., MD, 1/2 pay of a Pvt. 1817:29
  Pay to widow, Lethe, of WA co., MD, 1/2 pay of a Pvt., commencing from the date her husband's pension was paid up. 1824:25

Willmot, Robert - of Bourbon co., KY, 1/2 pay of a Lt. 1830:12

Wilmot, Robert, Revolutionary soldier, 1/2 pay of a Lt. of Artillery. rather than a Lt. of the line for the rest of his life. 1835:23

Wilson, David - of WA co., MD, 1/2 pay of a Pvt. 1819:45

Wilson, David - pay to Rachel Wilson, widow of David, late a pensioner of MD, arrears due on David's pension at the time of his death. 1828:24

Wimber, Thomas - of WO co., MD, 1/2 pay of a Pvt. 1827:11

Winbrough, Leah - widow of Thomas P. Winbrough, 1/2 pay of a Pvt. 1831:23

Wolcott, William - of Ohio , soldier of the Revolution, 1/2 pay of a Pvt. 1828:34

Wright, Ann - widow of Capt. Samuel T. Wright, 1/2 pay of a Capt. 1836:10

Wright, Edward - of KT co. MD, pay balance due, 11 lbs 5 sh, as a Lt. during the Revolutionary War. 1819:11

Wright, Jesse - an old soldier, 1/2 pay of a Pvt. 1812:38

Wycall (Wykall), Adam - Pay to his widow, Ann Martin of PG co., 1/2 pay of a Pvt. 1832:53

Wyndham, Sarah - , wid., of Annapolis, 1/2 pay of a Sgt. 1821:42
Pay Andrew Slicer of Annapolis, $20.83, amount [of pension] due Sarah Wyndham to Aug. 5, 1841, the day of her death. 1841:27

Yates, Thomas - to receive depreciation certificate and the Orphan's Court of AA co. is authorized to make a like provision as is directed by law, to be made to invalid pensioners. 1788:Res.

Young, Benjamin - of BA co., MD, 1/2 pay of a Sgt. 1816:26

A LIST OF THE NAMES OF PERSONS WHO

ARE ENTITLED TO RECEIVE A

PENSION

FROM THE STATE OF MARYLAND

December Session, 1822

Annapolis
1822

The following was copied from The
Maryland Historical Society *Pam. #2638

NAMES OF PERSONS

Anderson, Richard, Capt. ....
Benson, Perry, Capt. ....
Dawson, Joseph, Pvt. ....
Forrest, Rebecca, wid., U. F., Lt. Col. ....
Gambell, Abraham, Pvt. ....
Harman, Lazarus, Pvt. ....
Lavaschie, Ann, widow of Jno., Lt. ....

The following to be pd in virtue of their
respective orders drawn on the treasurer:

Allen, Jacob, Pvt. ....
Adams, Adam, Pvt. ....
Alvey, Josias, Pvt. ....
Anderson, John, Pvt. ....
Beall, D. William, Maj. ....
Bruel, William, Capt. ....
Bullock, Jesse, Pvt. ....
Beaver, Charles, Lt. ....
Boone, John, Lt. ....
Barrott, Solomon, Fifer ....
Bateman, George, Corp. ....
Burgess, Basil, Lt. ....
Bidwell, Richard, Pvt. ....
Bantham, Peregrine, Pvt. ....
Becroft, John, Pvt. ....
Bennett, John, Pvt. ....
Bailey, Thomas, Pvt. ....
Burns, John, Pvt. ....
Brashears, Ignatius, Pvt. ....
Beall, Elizabeth, wid. of L. Beall, Capt. ....
Brewer, S. Thomas, Sgt. ....
Branson, B. John, Pvt. ....
Bruff, Margaret, wid. of J. Bruff, Capt. ....
Bush, Joseph, Pvt. ....

Annual Pension	Laws / Res. Authorized	Last Date Paid
$240	Act Nov S 1785 cl7	Aug 1, 1822
	do	Nov 1, 1822
40	Res. 1791	Aug 1, 1822
360	Res. Oct 1780	Aug 1, 1822
24	Res. Nov 1791	Nov 1, 1812
40	Res. Apr 1792	Nov 1, 1821
160	Act Nov 1785 c52	Aug 1, 1822
40	Res. Nov 1812	Oct 2, 1822
40	Dec 1815	Jul 23, 1822
40	do	Oct 23, 1822
40	Dec 1817	Feb 13, 1819
300	Nov 1808	Sep 9, 1822
240	Nov 1812	Mar 30, 1822
40	do	Jan 1, 1813
160	Dec 1815	Jul 23, 1822
160	do	Jan 23, 1822
44	do	Oct 23, 1822
44	do	Oct 23, 1821
160	Dec 1816	Jan 27, 1818
40	do	Oct 27, 1818
40	do	May 3, 1821
40	do	Jan 27, 1822
40	Feb 19, 1819	Nov 20, 1822
40	do	Nov 19, 1822
40	Dec 1817	May 7, 1822
40	do	Oct 30, 1822
240	Nov 1812	Sep 30, 1822
60	do	Jul 2, 1822
240	Jan 20, 1820	Jul 20, 1821
40	Feb 12, 1820	Nov 12, 1822

NAMES OF PERSONS

Byas, William, Lt. ....
Bonigardner, William, Pvt. ....
Coin, Dominick, Pvt. ....
Campbell, George, (Rank not stated) ....
Crouch, Robert, Pvt. ....
Carney, Thomas, Pvt. ....
Clinton, Thomas, Fife Maj. ....
Cahoe, Thomas, Pvt. ....
Clarke, James, Matross ....
Carr, Hezekiah, Drummer ....
Crawford, Nehemiah, Sgt. ....
Clewley, Joseph, Pvt. ....
Connelley, Hugh, Senr, Pvt. ....
Cato, George, Pvt. ....
Coe, William, Matross ....
Courts, C. Eleanor, Surgeons's Mate ....
Chambers, Edward, Pvt. ....
Dawson, William, Pvt. ....
Denny, Augusta, wid. R. D., Capt. ....
Donally, Patrick, Pvt. ....
Dyer, Walter, Lt. ....
Davison, James, Pvt. ....
Davis, William, Pvt. ....
Dowing, Nathaniel, Pvt. ....
Due, James, Pvt. ....
Dixon, William, Pvt. ....
Davis, Samuel, Fifer ....
Davis, Thomas, Pvt. ....
Duffee, Thomas, Sgt. ....
Dunning, Butler, Pvt. ....
Duvall, Joseph, Pvt. ....
Duvall, Benjamin (of Elisha), Pvt. ....
Elliott, Robert, Pvt. ....
Ebbs, Emanuel, Pvt. ....
Fearson, Joseph, Pvt. ....

Annual Pension	Laws / Res. Authorized	Last Date Paid
$160	Feb 14, 1821	Nov 14, 1822
40	Feb 16, 1821	Aug 16, 1822
40	Res. Nov 1803	Jul 3, 1822
50	Nov 1800	Nov 1, 1812
40	Nov 1812	Jul 2, 1822
40	do	Apr 2, 1822
54	do	Jul 2, 1822
40	do	do
50	do	Jan 2, 1815
44	Res. May 1813	Aug 27, 1822
60	Dec. 1815	Jan 23, 1822
40	do	Jul 23, 1816
40	Dec 1816	Oct 27, 1822
40	Feb 19, 1819	Nov 19, 1822
50	Feb 12, 1821	Nov 12, 1822
240	Feb 16, 1821	Nov 16, 1822
40	do	Aug 16, 1822
40	Nov 1810	Nov 15, 1822
240	Dec 1814	Nov 1, 1822
40	Dec 1815	Jan 23, 1818
160	Dec 1816	Mar 19, 1819
40	do	Oct 27, 1822
40	do	Jul 27, 1822
40	Dec 1817	Aug 7, 1821
40	Feb 19, 1819	Aug 19, 1822
40	do	May 19, 1822
44	Feb 12, 1820	Nov 12, 1822
40	do	do
60	do	do
40	Feb 16, 1821	May 16, 1822
40	do	do
40	Feb 18, 1822	Feb 18, 1822
40	Res. Nov 1811	Jul 4, 1822
40	Dec 1815	Apr 27, 1822
40	Dec 1815	Apr 23, 1822

NAMES OF PERSONS

Frazier, Samuel, Pvt. ....
Frazier, Solomon, Capt. ....
Foggett, Richard, Pvt. ....
Frazier, Levin, 1st Lt. ....
Frazier, James, Pvt. ....
Foard, Hezekiah, Lt. ....
Gordon, Archibald, Pvt. ....
Gadd, Thomas, Pvt. ....
Gerrish, Edward, Pvt. ....
Goldsborough, Charles, Pvt. ....
Galworth, Gabriel, Pvt. ....
Griffith, Nathan, Pvt. ....
Gates, William, Pvt. ....
Gudgeon, William, Pvt. ....
Griffith, Samuel, Capt. ....
Griffith, Philemon, Major ....
Gray, George, Pvt. ....
Groves, William, Pvt. ....
Greentree, Benjamin, Pvt. ....
Gassaway, L. Elizabeth, Capt. ....
Gordon, Elizabeth, wid. of John, Pvt. ....
Grove, David, (rank not given) ....
Hopkins, David, Pvt. ....
Harvey, Zadock, Capt of Horse ....
Halkerstone, Robert, Pvt. ....
Hill, John, Pvt. ....
Harper, William, Pvt. ....
Hillman, William, Pvt. ....
Hook, Joseph, Corp. ....
Hooper, Abraham, Pvt. ....
Harrison, Kinsey, Pvt. ....
Hurdle, Lawrence, Sgt. ....
Hurst, Samuel, Pvt. ....
Hutson, John, Pvt. ....
Hanspan, John Codlep, Pvt. ....

Annual Pension	Laws / Res. Authorized	Last Date Paid
$ 40	Dec 1816	Jan 7, 1818
240	Feb 19, 1819	Aug 19, 1822
40	Feb 12, 1820	Aug 12, 1822
160	do	Aug 12, 1822
40	Feb 14, 1820	Aug 14, 1822
160	Feb 9, 1822	Aug 9, 1822
40	Nov 1807	Sep 5, 1802
40	Nov 1811	Jun 11, 1818
40	Nov 1812	Oct 2, 1822
40	Dec 1815	Jul 23, 1822
40	Dec 1816	Jul 27, 1822
40	do	Oct 27, 1822
40	Dec 1815	Jan 23, 1822
40	Feb 19, 1819	Nov 19, 1821
240	do	Nov 19, 1821
300	do	May 19, 1822
40	Feb 12, 1820	May 12, 1822
40	do	Aug 12, 1822
40	do	Nov 12, 1822
240	Feb 10, 1821	Nov 10, 1822
40	Feb 16, 1821	May 26, 1822
40	Feb 17, 1821	Nov 17, 1822
300	Nov 1803	Oct 15, 1822
40	Nov 1811	Oct 6, 1822
160	Dec 1817	Nov 7, 1822
40	Nov 1812	Jul 2, 1822
40	do	Jan 2, 1814
40	do	Apr 2, 1822
44	Dec 1815	Jul 23, 1822
40	Dec 1816	Jan 27, 1822
40	Res. Dec 1816	Jul 27, 1822
60	do	Oct 27, 1822
40	Dec 1817	Aug 7, 1822
40	Dec 1817	Nov 7, 1821
40	Dec 1817	Feb 7, 1818

NAMES OF PERSONS

Hewitt, James, Pvt. ....
Head, John, Pvt. ....
Hempston, William, Pvt. ....
Holland, Joseph, Pvt. ....
Holland, Jacob, Corp. Dragoons ....
Handy, Elizabeth, Capt. ....
Hazelip, Richard, Pvt. ....
Handy, Nancy, Capt. ....
Hood, Edward, Pvt. ....
House, Michael, Pvt. ....
Inreson, John, Pvt. ....
Johnson, Archibald, Sgt. ....
Jones, Neale, Pvt. ....
Jaquet, D. John, Sgt. ....
Jones, Aaron, Pvt. ....
Jacob, John J., Lt. ....
Jeffries, Jacob (East. Shore Treas.), Pvt. ....
Jones, William, Pvt. ....
Issable, Elizabeth, Sgt. ....
Jackson, Ann, Pvt. ....
King, Thomas, Sgt - Transferred to wife,
  Mary, Res. Nov. 1811 ....
Kershner, Michael, Pvt. ....
King, Henry, Commissary ....
Kindle, William, Pvt. ....
King, George, Pvt. ....
Kent, Isaac, Pvt. ....
Knight, Jacob, Pvt. ....
Kilty, Catherine, Capt of Horse ....
Lynch, Hugh, Pvt. ....
Langford, Elijah, Pvt. ....
Lucas, Basil, Sgt. ....
Lord, Andrew, Pvt. ....
Leather, John, Sgt. ....
Law, William, Pvt. ....

Annual Pension	Laws / Res. Authorized	Last Date Paid
$ 40	Feb 19, 1819	Feb 19, 1819
40	do	Aug 19, 1822
40	do	do
40	do	Nov 19, 1822
60	do	Nov 19, 1821
240	Feb 9, 1821	Aug 9, 1822
40	Feb 16, 1821	Feb 16, 1821
240	Feb 9, 1822	Aug 9, 1822
40	Feb 23, 1822	Aug 23, 1822
40	do	Nov 23, 1822
40	Res. Nov 1803	Oct 6, 1822
60	Nov 1812	Apr 2, 1818
40	do	Jan 2, 1820
60	Dec 1815	Jul 23, 1816
40	do	Jul 23, 1822
160	Dec 1816	Oct 27, 1822
40	do	
40	Feb 12, 1820	Aug 12, 1822
60	Feb 20, 1822	Nov 20, 1822
40	Feb 23, 1822	Nov 23, 1822
60	Jun 1809	Dec 10, 1811
40	Dec 1815	Jul 23, 1822
240	Dec 1817	Feb 13, 1820
40	do	Feb 7, 1818
40	Feb 19, 1819	May 9, 1822
40	Feb 12, 1820	Aug 12, 1822
40	do	Feb 12, 1820
300	Jan 4, 1822	Oct 4, 1822
40	Nov 1812	Jan 1, 1822
40	do	Oct 2, 1822
60	Dec 1815	Jan 28, 1822
40	do	Oct 25, 1822
60	Dec 1816	Jul 27, 1822
40	do	Jul 27, 1818

NAMES OF PERSONS

Layman, William, Lt. ....
Leonard, James, Pvt. ....
Lynn, Eleanor, wid. of John, Lt. ....
Lomax, John, Pvt. ....
Lewis, William, Sgt. ....
Lucas, John, Sgt. ....
Lloyd, Thomas, Pvt. ....
Lord, Henry, Pvt. ....
Mahoney, Edward, Pvt. ....
McCoy, John, (Rank not stated) ....
Mills, Cornelius H. (Rank not stated) ....
Milburn, Nicholas, Pvt. ....
M'Connell, Samuel, Sgt. ....
Magruder, Nathaniel B., Lt. ....
M'Pherson, Mark, Lt. ....
Medlar, Bostian, Drum Maj. ....
M'Kinsey, Moses, Drummer ....
M'Gee, William, Pvt. ....
M'Gee, Charles, Pvt. ....
Mahoney, Clement, Pvt. ....
Moutle/Moudle, George, Pvt. ....
M'Cann, Michael, Pvt. ....
Murdock, Benjamin, Lt. ....
Minitree, Paul, Pvt. ....
Mudd, Bennet, Sgt. ....
Moore, Rueben, Pvt. ....
M'Quinny, Thomas, Pvt. ....
Mayhew, Jonathan, Pvt. ....
Mills, Zachariah, Pvt. ....
Merrick, William, Corp. ....
Middleton, Sarah, Capt. ....
Nowell, James, Pvt. ....
Newman, John, Sgt. ....
Niblet, William, Pvt. ....
Newton, John, Pvt. ....

Annual Pension	Laws / Res. Authorized	Last Date Paid
$160	Dec 1816	Jan 27, 1822
40	Dec 1817	Feb 7, 1822
160	do	Aug 13, 1822
40	Feb 19, 1819	Aug 19, 1822
60	Feb 12, 1820	Feb 12, 1822
60	do	Aug 12, 1822
40	do	Nov 12, 1822
40	Feb 16, 1821	Nov 16, 1822
40	Nov 1811	Jul 4, 1818
125	do	Oct 6, 1822
125	do	Jul 6, 1822
40	Nov 1812	Jun 30, 1822
60	do	Jul 2, 1822
160	Dec 1815	Oct 23, 1821
160	do	Oct 23, 1822
54	do	Jan 23, 1816
44	do	Jul 23, 1822
40	do	do
40	do	Jan 23, 1822
40	do	Jan 23, 1816
40	Dec 1817	Aug 10, 1822
40	do	Nov 6, 1822
160	do	May 6, 1819
40	Feb 19, 1819	Nov 19, 1819
60	do	Feb 19, 1822
40	do	Aug 19, 1822
40	do	Aug 19, 1822
40	do	Feb 19, 1822
40	Feb 12, 1820	Nov 12, 1822
44	Feb 16, 1820	Nov 16, 1822
240	Feb 9, 1822	Nov 9, 1822
40	Nov 1812	Oct 2, 1822
60	Res. Dec 1816	Oct 27, 1822
40	do	Apr 27, 1822
40	Dec 1817	Aug 7, 1822

NAMES OF PERSONS

O'Conner, Michael, Matross . . . .
Orndorff, Christian, Capt. . . . .
Ott, Adam, Lt. . . . .
Proctor, Richard, Pvt. . . . .
Peacock, Neale, Pvt. . . . .
Powers, Jesse, Pvt. . . . .
Pindell, Richard, Surgeon . . . .
Pen, John, Pvt. . . . .
Philips, Stephen, Pvt. . . . .
Poe, Elizabeth, Capt. . . . .
Reading, Henry, Pvt. . . . .
Rowie, Thomas, Lt. . . . .
Richardson, Daniel, Pvt. . . . .
Richardson, Charles, Pvt. . . . .
Roberts, William, Pvt. . . . .
Roby, John, Pvt. . . . .
Reiley, William, Capt. . . . .
Robbins, John, Pvt. . . . .
Reynolds, Tobias, Pvt. . . . .
Ray, Joseph, Pvt. . . . .
Rigby, William, Quartermaster Sgt. . . . .
Richardson, Nancy, Pvt. . . . .
Rawlings, Anne, Pvt. . . . .
Second, George, Corp. . . . .
Seaburn, John, Pvt. . . . .
Spalding, Henry, Pvt. . . . .
Semmes, James, 2nd Lt. . . . .
Simpson, Rezin, Sgt. Dragoons . . . .
Spalding, Aaron, Sgt. . . . .
Stephens, Levi, Pvt. . . . .
Smith, Christian, Pvt. . . . .
Studer, Philip, Pvt. . . . .
Scott, Samuel, Pvt. . . . .
Stevens, Benjamin, Pvt. . . . .
Summers, Solomon, Drummer. . . . .

Annual Pension	Laws / Res. Authorized	Last Date Paid
$ 40	Nov 1812	Jan 2, 1822
240	Feb 19, 1891	Aug 19, 1822
160	Feb 22, 1822	Nov 22, 1822
40	Nov 1811	Oct 6, 1813
40	Nov 1812	Oct 2, 1822
40	Dec 1815	Jan 23, 1822
720	Dec 1816	May 25, 1822
40	Feb 16, 1821	Feb 16, 1822
40	do	May 16, 1822
240	Feb 9, 1822	Nov 9, 1822
40	Nov 1811	Dec 13, 1812
160	do	Dec 21, 1819
40	do	Oct 2, 1822
40	do	Jan 2, 1820
40	Dec 1815	Oct 23, 1822
40	do	Jul 23, 1818
240	Dec 1816	Oct 27, 1822
40	Dec 1817	Aug 7, 1822
40	do	do
40	do	May 7, 1822
60	Feb 12, 1820	Aug 12, 1822
40	Feb 16, 1821	May 16, 1822
40	Feb 23, 1822	Nov 23 1822
44	Nov 1803	[no date]
40	Nov 1811	Jun 21, 1812
40	do	Dec 21, 1821
160	Nov 1812	Oct 2, 1822
90	Dec 1815	Oct 27, 1822
60	do	Jan 23, 1821
40	do	Oct 23, 1821
40	do	Jul 23, 1822
40	do	do
40	Dec 1816	Aug 5, 1822
40	do	Oct 27, 1819
44	do	Oct 27, 1822

NAMES OF PERSONS

Simpson, Lawrence, Pvt. ....
Swann, Leonard, Pvt. ....
Sholts, John, Pvt. ....
Smith, Elijah, Pvt. ....
Sewall, James, Pvt. ....
Smith, John (AA Co.), Pvt. ....
Smith, John (CH Co.), Pvt. ....
Simmons, Aaron, Pvt. ....
Sewall, Charles, 1st Lt. ....
Spedden, Edward, 2nd Lt. ....
Staples, John, Pvt. ....
Sewell, William, Pvt. ....
Thompson, Jesse, Sgt. ....
Tutwiller, Jonathan, Sgt. ....
Taylor, Richard, Pvt. ....
Thompson, Charles, Pvt. ....
Townsend, Allen, Pvt. ....
Turner, Thomas, Pvt. ....
Tasker, Richard R., Pvt. ....
Tillard, Sarah, wid/Lt. Col. Taylor, Capt. ....
Thompson, Mary, Pvt. ....
Toonry, John, Corp. ....
Taylor, Mary, Pvt. ....
Thomas, Joseph (pd. to Frisby Henderson,
   Trustee of Thomas), Pvt. ....
Vaughn, William, Pvt. ....
Varlow, Stephen, Pvt. ....
Wilkinson, Young, Lt. Artillery ....
Williams, Charles, Pvt. ....
Wright, Jesse, Pvt. ....
Watkins, Leonard, Sgt. ....
Wilkinson, James, Col. Dragoons ....
Watkins, Gassaway, Capt. ....
Waters, Richard, Capt. ....

Annual Pension	Laws / Res. Authorized	Last Date Paid
$ 40	Dec 1816	Apr 27, 1822
40	Dec 1817	May 7, 1819
40	do	Nov 7, 1822
40	do	Nov 6, 1822
40	do	do
40	Feb 19, 1819	Aug 19, 1822
40	do	Feb 19, 1821
40	do	Feb 19, 1822
160	Feb 14, 1820	Aug 14, 1822
160	do	May 14, 1820
40	Feb 12, 1820	Feb 12, 1822
40	Feb 21, 1822	Aug 21, 1822
60	Nov 1812	Oct 1, 1822
60	Dec 1815	Apr 29, 1819
40	do	Jan 23, 1816
40	do	Jan 27, 1817
40	do	Jul 27, 1817
40	Feb 19, 1819	Nov 19, 1819
40	Feb 12, 1820	May 12, 1822
240	Jan 22, 1820	Jul 22, 1820
40	Feb 16, 1821	Aug 16, 1822
44	do	May 16, 1822
40	Feb 17, 1821	Aug 17, 1822
40	Feb 22, 1822	Feb 22, 1822
40	Nov 181-	Apr 2, 1822
40	Feb 12, 1820	Nov 12, 1822
200(1/2 yr)	Nov 1810	Jun 18, 1822
40	Nov 1812	Oct 1, 1822
40	do	Jan 2, 1816
60	do	Jul 2, 1822
562.50	Dec 1815	Oct 26, 1821
240	do	Oct 23, 1822
240	do	Oct 23, 1822

NAMES OF PERSONS

Williams, John, Corp. ....
White, George, Pvt. ....
Willis, Andrew, Pvt. ....
Wall, William, Pvt. ....
Waters, Jonathan, Pvt. ....
Walker, John, Corp. ....
Wilson, David, Pvt. ....
Wyndham, Sarah, Sgt. ....
Young, Benjamin, Pvt. ....
Uncles, Benjamin, Pvt. ....

248 pensioners

Annual Pension	Laws / Res. Authorized	Last Date Paid
$ 44	Dec 1815	Jul 23, 1822
40	Dec 1814	Nov 5, 1821
40	Dec 1817	Nov 7, 1822
40	Feb 19, 1819	Aug 19, 1822
40	...... do	Nov 19, 1822
44	Feb 16, 1821	Nov 16, 1822
40	...... do	do
60	Feb 22, 1822	Nov 22, 1822
60	Dec 1816	Jan 27, 1822
40	Feb 22, 1822	Aug 22, 1822
$19,822.50		

Treasury Office, Dec. 2, 1822

    Benjamin Harwood, T.W.S.M.*

*Treasurer, West Shore [of] Maryland

INDEX

A

Abbott, George 7, 91
Able, Cuthbert 7
Absolum, William 8
Ackworth, Lydia 134
Adams, Adam 7, 91, 152
  Ignatius 7
  Jacob 8
  John 7, 8
  Peter 1
  Thomas 8
  William 1
Addy, James 8
Alcock, Robert 91
Aldridge, Nathan 8
Alexander, Jacob 91
  Mary 91
  Thomas S. 70
Allen, Emanuel 7
  Jacob 91, 152
  James 7
  Nathan 91
  William 8
Alley, Barnet 8
Allison, Thomas 8
Alvey, John 7
  Josiah 8
  Josias 91, 152
  Thomas G. 8
  Travers 8
Amos, Elizabeth 91
Anderson, Archibald 1
  Daniel 7
  John 8, 91, 152
  Michael 8
  Richard 1, 91, 152
Andrews, John 7
Appleby, John 7
Armistead, John B. 72
  Walker K. 72
Armstead, L. A. 61
Armstrong, Anna Maria 70
  Edward 60
  George 1
  J. D. 61
  James 1
  James D. 84
  John 7, 8
Arrants, James 8
Arthur, Thomas 8
Ashbury, John 8
Ashby, John J. 61
Ashley, James 8
Ashmore, John 7
Aspin, Thomas 8
Asque, Peregrine 8
Auber, John 8
Auld, Daniel 91
  Sarah 91
Austin, Harris 8
  Henry 8, 44
Ayhern, William 7
Ayres, Elizabeth 92
  Frederick 8
  Thomas 7, 92

B

Baber, James 10
Bagues, Jacques 2
Bailey, James 10
  Philip 9
  Thomas 9, 152
Baily, Mountjoy 92
  Thomas 92
Baker, Henry 2
  Henry Cleland 92
  Joel 12
  John 8
  Thomas 10
Baldwin, Henry 1, 92
  Samuel 92
  William H. 92
Balip, James 11
Baliss, James 11
Ballard, Levin 129
Baltzel, Charles 92
  Jacob 92

Baltzell, Charles 2
Banneman, John 11
Banny, James 12
Bantham, John 10
  Peregrine 92, 152
Barber, Thomas 11
Barclay, Thomas 11
Barkholder, Christian 64
Barley, Nathaniel 12
Barnet, Robert 13, 14
Barnett, Jesse 10
  John 9
Barney, Moses 10
Barns, Nehemiah 13
Barret, Joshua 9
Barrett, John 9
  Joshua 92
  Solomon 10
Barron, James 9
Barrott, Solomon 92, 152
  Susan 92
Barrow, James 11
Bartley, Thomas 11
Barton, Joseph 10
Basil, Daniel 8
Basset, Richard 13
Batchely, Joshua 9
Bateman, George 8, 92, 152
  Nathan 11

Batten, William 11
Batton, Hugh 13
  John 13
Baxter, John 12
  Thomas 11
Bayley, James 12
  John 11
  Mountjoy 93
Beach, John 9
Beachy, Christian 60
  John 80
Beall, D. William 152
  Elizabeth 93, 111, 152
  Henrietta 93
  L. 152
  Lawson 93
  Lloyd 1, 93
  Samuel B. 2
  William D. 93
  William Dent 1
Bean, John 9
  Leonard 9, 93
Bear, Thomas 10
Beatty, Jane 93
  Thomas 2, 93
  William 1
Beaven, Charles 93
Beaver, Charles 152
Beck, Alexander 12, 13
  Simon 93

Beckett, Humphrey 10
Beckwith, Nehemiah 93
Becroft, John 93, 152
Beekman, John 78
Belcher, Benjamin 12
Belfast, George 11
Belt, John Sprigg 1, 93, 113
Bennet, John 11, 13
Bennett, Frederick 9, 93
  John 94, 152
Benny, John 12, 13
Benson, Joseph 94
  Mary 94
  Perry 1, 94, 152
Berriman, John 11
Berry, Edward 11, 94
  James 12
  Zachariah 11
Bewley, George 94
  Grace 94
Biass, James 9
Biddle, Richard 10
Bidwell, Richard 94, 152
Biggs, John 11
Bigwood, James 10
Billop, Henry 10
Bird, Richard 1

Bird, Thomas 9
Bishop, Jane 94, 107
  Thomas 11
Black, Harrison 78
Blackham, George 9
Blades, John 9
Blair, John 9, 12
Blaize, Joseph 10
Blake, Jacob 11
  John 94
  Patsy 94
Blansford, Richard 11
Blewer, James 11
Bluer, James 94
Bochard, Peter 9
Body, Robert 13
Bohrer, Maria 108
Bolton, John 94
  William 12, 13
Bomgardner, Margaret 94
  William 94
Bond, John 95
Bonham, Malachai 2
Bonigardner, William 154
Boody, John 12
Boon, Joseph 138
Boone, John 95, 152
  Richard 10
Boswell, Jesse 10

Boswell, Samuel 11
Botts, Joseph 10
Boudy, John 12
Bough, Benjamin 12
  George 11
Bowe, George 13
Bowen, Abram 10
  James 12
  Jehu 95
  Robert 9
Bowers, George 12, 95
Bowler, Peter 9
  Thomas 11
Bowles, Martin 10
  William 12
Bowser, Thomas 10
Boyd, Benjamin 9
  Thomas 1
Boyer, Michael 1, 95
Boyle, James 13
Boyles, Daniel 12
Bracco, Bennett 95
Bradley, George 9
Brady, John 11
  Thomas 10
  William 12
Braithwait, William 11
Bramble, Andrew 12
  David 12
  Levin 9
Brand, Gabriel 9

Brannan, James 11
  Laurence 10
Branson, B. John 152
  John 10
  John B. 95
  Mary 95
Brant, John 63
Brashears, Ignatius 95, 152
Bray, Henry 62
  John 62
  Philip H. 61
  Richard 61
Brent, John 9
Brevett, John 2
Brewer, John 10
  S. Thomas 152
  Susanna 95
  Thomas 95
  Thomas S. 95
Brian, John 11
Brice, Jacob 1
  John 59, 62, 65, 69, 71, 73
  Julianna 95
Bright, William 13
Briley, John 12
Britain, Joseph 2
Britt, Robert 12, 95
Brittenham, Solomon 9
Britton, George 96
  John 12
  Joseph 96

Broadwater,
  Jefferson 78
  William 68, 85
Brookbank, John 8
Brookes, William 8
Brookhart, David 112
Brooks, Benjamin 1
  Elizabeth 96, 136
Broome, Thomas 13
Brown, Basil 9
  George 9, 10
  James 12, 13, 122
  Jeremiah 10
  John 9, 10, 11, 13
  Joshua 10
  Lydia 116
  Thomas 9, 11
  William 1, 13
Browning, Meshach 81
  Meshack 62, 66, 73
Bruce, Robert 85, 96
  Upton 85
  William 1, 96
Bruel, William 152
Bruff, J. 152
  James 1, 96
  Margaret 96, 152
  William 12
Bryan, Charles 96

Bryan, James 11
Bryant, James 96
Buchanan, John 9
Buck, George 10
Buckley, Daniel 9
  John 9
  Thomas 8
Buckliss, Charles 11
Bulger, Daniel 10
Bullock, Jesse 96, 152
Bumgardner, George 10
Burch, Benjamin 10, 11, 96
  Joseph 11
  Thomas 12
  Zachariah 9
Burell, Samuel B. 62
Burgess, Basil 2, 96, 152
  Joseph 1, 10
  Joshua 2, 96, 97
  Vachel 97
  William 11
Burk, Elizabeth 97
  James 10
  Levi 8
  Nathaniel 97
Burnes, Ezekiel 12
  Harvey 13
  John 12
  Luke 12
Burns, Hugh 12

Burns, John 97, 152
  Michael 12, 13
Burroughs, Eleanor Turner 97
  Norman 97
Burtham, Perry 9
Burton, Isaac 11
Busey, Anne 97
Bush, Joseph 97, 152
Bushell, Peter 10
Butcher, John 11
Butler, Richard 9
Butt, Barruch 8
  Edward 8, 97
  Thomas 8, 97
Buttery, Thomas 12, 13
Button, Levy 9
Butts, Zachariah 12
Buxton, Abijah 10
Byas, William 97, 154
Byrn, Charles 12
Byus, William 97

C

Cadle, Ann 97
Cahill, Timothy 16
Cahoe, Thomas 15, 97, 154
Caile, David 14
Cain, Edward 17
  Hugh 14
Callahan, John 98

Callahan, Robert 15
Samuel 16
Sarah 98
Callhan, Michael 14
Calmes, George 59, 61, 63, 66, 67, 73, 77, 81, 82
Campbell, George 98, 154
John 18
Nicholas 19
Robert 17, 18
Campfield, Sarah 111
Camphen, John 14
Campher, Thomas 14
Canfield, Thomas 98
Cann, Augustine 15
William 18
Cannady, Thomas 16
Cannon, John 17
Carberry, Peter 16
Cardiff, Thomas 17
Carey, Owen 15
Carleton, John M. 80
Carlile, John 2
Carlin, Mary 98
William 98
Carmile, Calothile 16
Carnant, Jacob 16
Carnes, Kobert 17
Carney, George 17
Thomas 15, 98, 154
Carns, Arthur 17
Benajamin 18
Carr, Hezekiah 14, 98, 154
Ingram 98
John 15, 98
Margaret 98
Michael 18
Stephen 15
Carrick, Joseph 35
Carroll, Bryan 17
John 14, 15
Carson, John 2, 16
Carter, John 16
Justinian 18
Luke 14
Samuel 17
William 16
Cartro, William 14
Carvin, James 99
Carwell, Peter 18
Cary, John 2
Casey, James 16
Peter 18
William 15
Casner, Michael 16
Cassaday, Barney 18
Casson, Philip 99
Catchsides, Abram 14
Cathagone, Emanuel 14
Cato, George 99, 154
William 14
Cavenaugh, Patrick 14
Caves, John 18
Cecil, Barton 14
Cernish, John 18
Chamber, Edward 17
Chambers, Edward 99, 154
James 17
Chaplin, Hugh 17
Chapman, Henry 2
Henry H. 99
Mary 99
Thomas 18, 99
William 15
Chapple, Samuel 16
Chappoik, Simon 18
Chard, James 17
Charles, Jacob 132
Charlton, John Usher 99
Chatland, William 14
Cheser, Bennet 18
Cheshire, John 15
Chesley, Robert 99
Chestnut, Benjamin 19

Chestnut, William 19
Chever, John 2
Childs, George 14
Chinn, Samuel 18
Chisholm,
  Archibald 81
  James 64
Chitham, Aquilla 15
Chubb, Jonathan 15
Citizen, Morris 14
Civill, William 16
Clagett, Jane 130
Clagget, Ami 99
  Samuel 99
Claggett, Horatio 2
  John 14
Clancey, John 16
Claney, Daniel 14
  Edward 15
  Michael 15, 18
Clapper, Valentine 16
Clark, John 17
  Michael 14
  Samuel 18
  Thomas 14
  Zachariah 18
Clarke, George 15
  James 17, 99, 154
  John 19
  Richard 19
  Thomas 17

Clary, William 13, 14
Claus, Frederick 80
Cleaver, Benjamin 15
Clements, Andrew 64
  Bennet 74, 83
  Bennet H. 16
  Charles 14
  Henry 2
  James 18
  Thomas B. 14
  William 14, 16
Clemmahan, Robert 15
Cleverdence, John 17
Clewley, Joseph 100, 154
Clinton, Thomas 14, 100, 154
Cobb, Kindall 16
Cochran, Jame 17
  James 100
  John 15
Cochrane, Ann
  Mary 100
  James 100
Cockendall, Elijah 16
Cockey, Peter 2
Coe, Alexander
  Benson 100
  George C. 100
  Mary 100

Coe, Richard 100
  William 18, 100, 154
Coffeild, Owen 17
Coffin, Arthur 17
Coffroth, Conrad 100, 101
  Magdalena 101
Coin, Dominick 154
Coins, Dominick 16
Cole, Benjamin 16
  John 17, 18
  Michael 14
Colegate, Asaph 101
  Aseph 15
Coleman, Isham 16
  Nicholas D. 97
  Patten 101
Colin, John 14
Collard, James 14
Collier, William 18
Collins, George 17
  Jacob 17
  James 17
  John 17, 19
Collis, William 15
Compton, Edward 2
  Ignatius 15
  John 17
  Thomas 17
Condrum, Thomas 17

Connelley, Hugh 154
Connelly, Hugh 19, 101
  John 16, 18
  Priscilla 101
  Timothy 17
  William 101
Conner, David 14
  James 18
  Michael 17
  Patrick 18
  William 14
Cook, William 15
Cooke, Henry 101
Cooley, Joseph 16
  Robert 18
Coomy, John 19
Cooper, Charles 16
  John 16
  Thomas 15
  William 101
Cork, William 17
Cornick, Robert 15
Cornwell, William 17
Corr, Michael 18
Cosgrove, Edward 16
Cougleton, William 18
Coursey, Hamton 14
  William 18
Courts, C. Eleanor 154

Courts, Eleanor C. 101
  John 14
  Richard Hanley 101
Cousin, N. P. 142
Cowan, John 78
Coward, Nancy 101
  William 101
Cox, James 101
  John 18
  Josua 17
  Mary 101
  William 15, 102
Coyle, Michael 17
Coyn, Dominick 101, 122
  Mary 101, 122
Crady, David 16
Cragan, Dennis 16
Craig, James 2
  John 14, 19
  Thomas 16
Craigs, George 16
Craile, William 15
Crain, Peter W. 138
Craine, Henry 15
Crampton, Thomas 102
Crasbie, Jesse 19
Crasbury, James 18
Crawford, Jacob 2
  James 16
  Nehemiah 102, 154

Cresap, Joseph 102
  Robert 71
  S. 71
Croft, Catharine 102
  William 102
Crook, William 15
Crosby, John 16
Cross, Joseph 2
  Mary 102
  Robert 102
Crouch, Charles 15
  Hannah 102
  Joseph 17
  Robert 19, 102, 154
Crow, Adam 15
Crowley, Darby 15
Croxall, Charles 2, 102
Crozier, James 16
  John 18
Crummy, Andrew 15
Cullamine, Joseph 18
Cummins, William 15
Cunningham, J. 69
  James 66, 68, 71, 77
  Lewis 16
  Peter 18
Curl, John 17
Curren, James 15
Curritt, John 18

Curtis, John 102
  Michael 16
Cusick,
  Charistopher
  15
Cutler, William 14
Cyphart, Matthias
  18

D

Daffin, James 19
Daley, Thomas 21
Davidson, James
  20, 102
  John 2
Davis, Charles 21
  John 21, 22, 76,
  102
  Margaret 102
  Peter 21
  Rezin 2
  Robert 19
  Samuel 20, 102,
  103, 154
  Thomas 21, 103,
  154
  William 21, 103,
  154
Davison, James 154
Dawkins, Charles
  19, 103
  Elizabeth 103
Dawson, James 21
  Joseph 103, 152
  William 21, 103,
  154

Day, William 20
Deakin, Pearce 20
Deakins, John 20
  William 22
Deal, George 103
Deale, Joseph 22
Deane, Charles 21
  Elijah 19
  John 2, 21
Deaver, Aquilla 19,
  103
  Sarah 104
  William 20, 104
Deavor, Thomas 22
Deford, John 21
  Joseph 20
Degazoon, Peter 19
DeKalb, Baron 104
Delanaway, John
  20
Dempsey, Luke 19
Dennis, Edward
  104
Dennison, James 20
Dennsion, Patrick
  22
Denny, Augusta
  104, 154
  R. D. 154
  Robert 2, 104
  Samuel 20
Denoon, John 104
Denson, John 19,
  20
Dent, Eleanor 104
  George 104

Dent, John 20, 104
Denwood, Levin 2
Derrington,
  William 20
Deveaux, Butoc 20
Devecmon, George
  W. 68
  John 70
Devereux, James
  20
Devicman, Peter 89
Devine, William 20
Devit, George 20
Dias, George 21
Dice, George 21
Dickins, Edward A.
  79
Dickison, Thomas
  21
Disharoon, Thomas
  21
Divine, James 21
Dixon, George 19
  Henry 19
  John 19
  Richard 20
  William 19, 21,
  104, 154
Dobson, Henry 2
  John 21
Dohorty, Barnably
  21
Dolvin, Richard 21
Dominick, Beryer
  20
  Edward 20

Donagan, John 20
Donally, Elizabeth 104
  Patrick 104, 154
Donnelly, Elizabeth 104
  Patrick 104
Donohoe, Joseph 20
Donovan, John 19
  Richard 2
  Timothy 21
Doran, Patrick 20
Dorgan, John 105
Dorrent, John 105
Dorsey, Ely 105
  Richard 2, 105
Dortch, William 19
Dotrow, John 105
Dougherty, Edmund 19
Douglas, James 21
Douley, William 22
Dove, John 20
Dowden, James 20
Dowdle, William 22
Dowing, Nathaniel 154
Dowlan, Michael 22
Downes, William 19
Downey, Alexander 20
  John 19
Downing, Butler 105
Downing, Elizabeth 105
  Nathaniel 105
Downs, Richard 20
Doyle, James 19
  Terrane 89
  Thomas 19
Drane, George 66
  Marone 84
  Mary Ann 84
  Richard 80
  William 83
Drian, James 21
Driskill, Jeremiah 21
Drudge, Thomas 19
Drune, Richard 64
Duders, Jacob 21
Due, James 105, 154
Duffee, Bridget 105
  Thomas 105, 154
Duffy, Francis 21
  Michael 21
  Terrence 21
  Thomas 21
Dugan, Abram 21
Duhague, John 19
Dunar, Francis 19
Dunby, Richard 21
Duncan, Robert 20
Dunning, Butler 105, 154
  Dennis 19
Dunnington, Francis 19
Dunnington, William 20
Dunston, Peter 21
Dure, James 20
Durgan, Patrick 21
Dutton, Thomas 20, 21
Duval, Joseph 106
Duvall, Benjamin 106, 154
  Edward 2
  Elisha 106
  Isaac 2
  Joseph 154
  Richard 19
Duvist, Francis 20
Dyche, Matthias 20
Dyer, Edward 2
  George 21
  James 20
  John 19
  Walter 2, 106, 154
Dyson, Thomas A. 2

E

Earlougher, Sarah 144
Easom, Mary 148
Easton, Sarah 106, 114
Ebbs, Emanuel 23, 106, 154
Eccleston, Jarvis 22
Eddy, James 8

Edelin, John 106
  Raphael C. 110
Edes, James 23
Edgerly, Edward 3, 106
Edminston, Samuel 3
Edquidowney, Peter 22
Edwards, Heathesat 22
  John 22, 23
  Thomas 22
Eisell, John 106
Elbert, John L. 3
Elkins, William 22
Ellicott, Edward 22
  John 22
  Joseph 22
  Thomas 22
Elliott, Nicholas 23
  Robert 106, 154
  Thomas 22, 106
Ellis, Michael 22, 107
  Richard 23
  Thomas 22
  William 22
Ellison, Richard 23
  Thomas 23
Elliss, Thomas 107
Elms, George 22
Emory, Charles 107
Enlow, Jacob 85
Ennis, Enork 22

Ennis, John 22
  Leonard 22, 94, 107
Ervine, Edward 23
  James 23
Esom, Bartholomew 22
Etheridge, John 23
Evans, Benjamin 23
  Edward 22
  Eleanor 107
  Elijah 3
  Euel 23
  Henry 22
  James 22
  John 23
  Peregrine 22
  Samuel 22
  Thomas 22, 107
  William 22
Ewing, James 3, 107
Eyen, Frederick 23

F

Fairbank, John 25
Fairbrother, Francis 23, 107
  Patience 107
Fairburn, William 25
Fanning, Thomas 25
Farara, Emanuel 24
Fardo, Absolum 24

Farmer, Samuel 3
Farraby, Richard 23
Farrel, James 23
  Robert 24
  Walter 24
Farrell, John 23
  Peter 25
  William 24
Fearson, Joseph 107, 154
Feckel, Benjamin 3
Feike, John 68
Fellason, George 23
Fenlayson, George 23
Fennel, Edward 25
  John 25
Fennell, Stephen 24, 107
Fenwick, Richard 25
Ferguson, John 23
  Robert 62
Fernan, Andrew 25
Fickle, Benjamin 107
Fields, George 25
Filmont, Doras 24
Filson, Samuel 24
Finchham, Edward 24
Finley, Ebenezer 3
  John 24
Firth, Robert 25

Fisher, Henry 23, 25
Joseph 25
Philip 24
William 23
Fitzgerald,
  Benjamin 24, 107
  Charles 24
  Nicholas 24, 107
  William 24
Fitzhugh, Peregrine 7
  William 7, 108
Fitzjerald, James 23
  Jeremiah 25
  John 25
Fitzpatrick, Nathan 108
  Philip 24
Flack, James 25
Flannigan, Dennis 24
Fleckinger, Abraham 69
Flemming, Thomas 25
Fling, James 108
  James W. 108
Flinon, Frederick 23
Flood, James 25
Flora, Jacob 23
Flowers, Edmund 25

Flowers, Edward 24
Fluart, Massey 25
Fluhart, Stephen 24
Foard, Hezekiah 156
Foggett, Arthridge 108
  Richard 108, 156
Folger, Roger 24
Folling, John 24
Folliot, Banjamin 24
  Joseph 25
Ford, Benjamin 3
  George 24
  Hezekiah 3, 108
  Mary 108
  Robert 25
Foreman, William 24
Forest, Rebecca 108
Forrest, Rebecca 152
  U. F. 152
  Uriah 3
Forster, James 23
  Mark 24
  Moses 24
Fosdale, Stafford 23
Fosset, John 24
Foster, Rigby 24
Fountain, Peter 24

Fountain, William 25
Fowler, Henry 133
  Jonathan 23
  Joseph 23
Fox, Anthony 108
Foxall, David 24
  Thomas 24
Francis, Alexander 23
Franeway, John 23
Franklin, John 25
  William R. 23
Frantz, John 69
  Joseph 69
Frawney, John 24
Frazier, Elizabeth 109
  Fames 109
  Henrietta M. 108
  James 108, 156
  Levin 109, 156
  Penelope 109
  Samuel 25, 109, 156
  Solomon 109, 156
  Susan 109
  William 108
Freeman, Francis 23
  Richard 23
Freemoutt, Robert 25
French, Jeremiah 24

French, Peter 24
  William 25
Fresh, Stephen 23
Freshwater,
  Benjamin 25
Friend, Nicholas 80
  Samuel 80
Frumley, Thomas 25
Fulford, John 25
Fulham, Charles 25
  John 24
Funner, John M. 24
Furriner, Edward 23

G

Gadd, Thomas 27, 109, 156
Gainer, Hugh 26
Gaither, Ephriam 75
  George 75
  Henry 3
Gale, Edward 3
  John 3
Gallaher, John 109
Galloway, Marshall 27
Galworth, Gabriel 109, 156
Gambell, Abraham 110, 152
Gamble, Abraham 26

Gambrel, Gideon 110
Gambrill, Maria 92
Games, Jacob 27
Ganet, Enoch 28
Gantt, Benjamin L. 106, 136
Garcena, Abraham 25
Garish, Edward 26
Garnet, Andrew 26
Garnett, Benjamin 3
Garth, James 26
Gassaway,
  Elizabeth L. 110
  Henry 3, 110
  John 3, 110
  L. Elizabeth 156
  Nicholas 3
Gater, Banjamin 27
Gates, William 26, 110, 156
Gather, John 27
Gatting, Sylvester 28
Gee, John 27
  Richard 26
Gelhampton,
  Robert 27
Geohagan, Anthony 26
George, Bennet 27
  Southy 27
  William 27

Gerrish, Edward 110, 156
Gerry, Samuel 26
Gibbart, Peter 110
Gibson, John 26
  Jonathan 3
  Woolman I. 141
Gilbert, Benjamin 27
Gilby, Henry 26
Giles, John 28
Gilham, Thomas 27
Gill, Jonathan 28
Gillispie, William 27
Gillon, Thomas 26
Gilpin, William 110
Girdler, Charles 27
Gist, John 3
  Mordecai 3
Glascow, William 26
Glasgow, Walter 28
Glass, Joseph 77
  Moses 77
Gleeson, Thomas 28
Glory, William 26
Glover, Thomas 26
Goddard, Benjamin 110
  John 26, 110
Godman, Samuel 111
Goff, Charles 27

Goldsborough, Ann 111
  Charles 26, 111, 156
  Henry 26
  Mark 28
  William 3
Goldsmith, Harriet 111
  Thomas 111
Gomber, John 111
Gon, John 69
Goodwin, James 27
Goody, Lambert 27
Goostry, Rubin 26
Gordon, Archibald 111, 156
  Elizabeth 111, 156
  John 26, 28, 111, 156
  Joseph 26
Gorman, John 26
Gossage, Thomas 26
Gould, James 3
  Sarah 111
  William 26, 111
Grace, Jesse 26
  Richard 3
Graham, John 27
  Philip 27
Grahame, Moses 26
Grant, William 27
Graves, Isaac 26
  Moses 28

Gravey, James 27
Gray, Benjamin 25
  George 111, 156
  Harvey 28
  Jacob 27
  James 26
  James Woolford 3
  Richard 28
  Samuel 27
  Vincent 27
  Wilson 27
Gree, Amos 25
Green, Ann 108
  Elizabeth 111
  Henry 26, 111
  Isaac 26
  John 25, 27
  Joseph 27
  Samuel 25
Greenage, William 27
Greene, Robert 68
  Solomon 27
Greentree, Benjamin 111, 156
  Mary 111, 112
Greenwood, James 26
Greer, Smart 27
Gregory, John 27
Grenard, Paul 26
Grey, Thomas 27
Grier, Zedikaiah Walley 145

Griffin, Mark 26
  Nathan 26, 112
  William 25
Griffith, Amos 27
  Nathan 156
  Philemon 112, 156
  Ruth 112
  Samuel 112, 156
Grimes, William 28
Grindage, William 60
Gromith, Jacob 3
Groom, Charles 28
Grósh, Michael 27
Grove, Catharine 112
  David 112, 156
  Mary 112
  William 112
Groves, William 27, 112, 156
Gudegon, William 112
Gudgeon, Benjamin 112
  William 27, 156
Gudgington, William 103
Gunby, John 3
Gwinn, John 112
Gwyn, Julia 112
Gwynn, John 26

H

Hackett, John 28
Hadder, Nehemiah 32
Haden, George 30
  John 31
Hafley, Mary Magdalena 113
  Stephen 113
Hagan, James 30
  Leonard 30
  Raphael 29
Hagarthy, George 30
Hagen, Walter 30
Haley, Calib 29
Halkerson, Robert 113
Halkerstone, Robert 113, 156
Hall, Daniel 33
  Edward 4
  John 28, 31
  Joseph 31
  Josiah C. 3
  Richard 31, 97, 113
Hallen, William 28
Halleron, James 30
Hamilton, Edward 4
  George 3, 31
  John 3, 31
  John A. 4, 113

Hamilton, Margaret 113
  Samuel 31
  William 29
Hammett, James M. K. 124
Hammond, Ed. 32
  Elizabeth 113
  James 29
  Thomas 33
  William 32
Hamston, William 30
Hancock, John 32
  Stephen 32
Handy, Anne G. 113
  Elizabeth 113, 158
  George 4, 113
  Isaac 113
  Levin 113
  Nancy 113, 158
Haney, Barney 31
  John 31
  Susanna 113
  William 33, 113
Hannan, John 29
Hanson, Isaac 4, 114
  Samuel 3
  William 4
Hanspan, John Cadlep 114
  John Codlep 156

Harding, Henry 108, 147
  Robert 28
Hardman, Henry 4
  John 3
Hardy, Elias 29
Hare, James 30
  John 30
Harley, Henry 32
Harling, Cornelius 28
Harman, Lazarus 152
Harmon, Lazarus 32, 114
Harper, Bethula 114
  Elizabeth 114
  Joseph 32
  Nathan 31
  Richard 28, 29
  Samuel 32
  William 28, 32, 114, 156
Harpham, Robert 31
Harrell, John 31
Harrington, Levin 32
  Richard 32
  Samuel 109
Harris, Arthur 3, 114
  Benton 33
  Henry 29
  James 29, 32

Harris, John 31, 33
  Richard 114
  Solomon 114
  Thomas 30, 31
  William 29, 30, 33
Harrison, Elisha 4
  Kinsey 114, 156
  Robert H. 114
  Samuel 31
  Thomas 33
  William 32
Hart, Thomas 28
Hartman, Michael 32
  William 29
Hartshorn, John 4, 114
Harty, Frederick 31
Harvey, Charles 31
  Daniel 29
  Joshua 33
  Matthew 33
  William 75
  Zadoc 114
  Zadock 30, 156
Harwood, Julia Ann 104
Haslip, John B. 30
  Ricard N. 28
Hatkerston, Robert 3
Hatton, David 30
Hawke, Michael 29
Hawkins, Henry 4

Hawman, Elizabeth 115
  Frederick 115
  Philip 115
Hawson, Thomas 32
Hayes, Richard 29
Haynes, John 30
Haynie, Ezekiel 4
Hays, John 115
  John H. 115
  Theresa 115
  Vachel 30
Haywood, Thomas 115
Hazelip, Richard 115, 158
Head, John 29, 115, 158
Heath, --- (Gen.) 117
  Charles 28
Heaton, Elizabeth 115
  James 33, 115
Hedge, William 32
Hellen, William 28
Hemphill, Joseph 33
Hempston, Nathan T. 115
  William 115, 158
Henderson, David 33
  Frisby 143, 164

Hendrickson, James 28
Hennisee, Edward 30
Herrginton, William 29
Hewitt, James 32, 115, 158
Hick, William 31
Hickell, Abijah 33
Hickens, John 32
Hickenson, William 33
Hickey, Charles 29
Higgens, John 30
Higgs, Henry 29
  Lazarus 30
Hill, Ann 116
  Charles 30
  George 33, 115
  Isaac 29
  James 29
  John 115, 156
  Philip 3
  Richard 116
  Thomas 32
  William 32
Hillary, John 30
Hilleary, William 75
Hillery, Rignel 4
Hillman, Biddy 116
  Sally 116
  William 31, 116, 156
Hiner, Nicholas 32

Hines, Henry 30
  Isaac 28
  Jacob 29
Hodibuck, Conrad 28
Holder, John 31
Holdman, Daniel 32
Holland, Edward 31, 116
  Jacob 116, 158
  James 116
  John 116
  Joseph 116, 158
  Mary 116
Holliday, Isaac 30
  John 31, 33
Hollis, Pompey 30
Hollydyoak, John 116
Holmes, John 29
Holston, John 29
Holt, Leonard 32
Holton, George 30
Homes, James 32
Hood, Edward 116, 158
  Isaiah 116
  James 116
  John 30
  Kitty 116
Hook, Joseph 116, 156
Hoole, Joseph 28
Hooper, Abraham 117, 156

Hooper, Jeremiah 28
Hoops, Adam 4, 117
Hope, Ralph 32
  William 32
Hopkins, David 4, 117, 156
  Francis 31
  James 33
  John 32
Horner, Frances 117
  Gustavus 117
Horney, William 31, 117
Horsefield, Joseph 31
Hoskins, --- (Mrs.) 117
  Randall 117
  Randolph 30, 117
Houk, Adam 127
House, Christiana 117
  Michael 117, 158
Housley, John 31
Howard, Austen 31
  Benjamin 117
  Cornelius 30
  John 28, 29, 117
  John Eager 117
  John Egar 3
  Peregrine 31
  Peter 30
Howe, Daniel 32

Howe, Walter 31
  William 29
Howell, John 29
  Lewis 79
Hoye, Elizabeth H. 85
  J. 76, 78, 84, 85, 86, 88
  John 60, 61, 63, 64, 65, 67, 68, 70, 71, 72, 73, 74, 81, 84
  Samuel 85
  Thomas 30
  William W. 63, 76, 78, 82, 84, 85, 86, 87, 88
Hubbard, David 60
Hudson, Elizabeth 118
  James 32
  John 32, 118
Huggens, Richard 32
Huggins, Samuel 33
Hughes, John 29
  Michael 28
  Samuel 29, 30
  William 30
Hughs, --- (Mrs.) 118
  John 118
Hugo, Samuel B. 91
Hugon, Thomas 4
Hukell, Joseph 31

Hulet, John 31
Hull, John 31
  Nathaniel 30
Hulls, John 28
Humphries, James 29
Hunt, Jacob 31
  John S. 30
Hurdle, Lawrence 29, 118, 156
Hurley, John 32
  Josiah 28
  Richard 29
  William 31
Hurst, Samuel 32, 118, 156
Huster, Nicholas 30
Huston, Phillip 31
Hutchcraft, Thomas 29
Hutcheson, William 32
Hutchings, Hercules 29
Hutson, John 29, 118, 156
Hutt, Elijah 32
Hutton, James 29
  William 28
Hyde, John 31

I

Ijams, Frederick 34
Imeson, John 118
Ingles, William 34
Inreson, John 158
Ireland, George 118
  John 34
  Mary 118
Irons, John 34, 63
Irvin, Edward 33
Irvine, Abram 34
Isaacs, James 34
  Joseph 34
Isabell, Elizabeth 118
Issable, Elizabeth 158
  Robert 33

J

Jackson, Ann 118, 158
  Ed. 34
  James 34
  John 34
  Priscilla 109
Jacob, John J. 62, 113, 118, 119, 158
Jacobs, Henry 33
  Jesse 34
  William 119
  Zachariah 33
James, Leonard 119
Jameson, Adam 34
Jamison, Adam 4
Jaquet, D. John 158
  John D. 119

Jarvis, Daniel 34
  John 35
Javins, Daniel 34
Jay, Martha 119, 139
Jeans, Joseph 34
Jeffers, Jacob 34
Jeffries, Jacob 119, 158
Jenkins, Joseph 33
  Richard L. 140
  Samuel 35
  Sarah 119
  Thomas 119
Jennings, George 34
Jewell, William 73, 83
Jinkins, William 34
Johns, Thomas 34
Johnson, Archibald 119, 158
  Eleanor 63
  John 63
  Nicholas 119
  Rebecca 119
Johnston,
  Archibald 33
  Benedict 34
  Benjamin 34
  Edward 80
  Francis 34
  Isaac 33
  John 33, 34
  Joseph 34
  Nicholas 119

Johnston, Rebecca 119
  Robert 33, 34
  Thomas 35
  William 33, 119
Joice, William 33
Jones, Aaron 34, 119, 158
  Charles 34
  Cotter 120
  David 33
  George 34
  John 34
  John Courts 4
  Joseph 33, 34
  Lillias M. 120
  Nancy 120
  Neale 120, 158
  Nealy 33
  Philip 34
  Samuel 120
  Solomon 120
  Thomas 33, 34, 120
  William 34, 35, 120, 158
Jordan, John 4, 35, 106

K

Karns, Benjamin 35
Kearns, Francis 36
  Thomas 36
Kearsey, Edward 35
Keckland, James 35
Keech, Walter 35
Keene, Samuel Y. 4
Keener, Christian 126
Kellow, William 35
Kelly, David 35
  Dennis 35
  Jacob 35
  James 35
  Martha 120
  Matthew 36
  Patrick 120
  William 120
Kelson, George 35
Kemble, Stephen 35
Kennard, John 36
Kennedy, David 36
  William 36
Kent, Isaac 120, 158
Kephart, Adam 35
Kernon, Michael 35
Kerrick, Benjamin H. 35
Kershner, Mary A. 121
  Mary Ann 120
  Michael 121, 158
Kettle, Abram 36
  David 36
Kidd, John 35
Kildee, John 35
Killigan, James 36
Killman, Edward 35

Kilty, Catharine 121
  Catherine 158
  John 4, 121
  William 4
Kincade, John 36
  Peter 35
Kindle, William 35, 121, 158
King, Cassandra Ann 135
  George 121, 158
  Henry 121, 158
  John 35
  Levin 121
  Margaret 121
  Mary 121, 158
  Thomas 35, 121, 158
  William 35
Kirk, Edward 36
Kisby, Richard 36
Kiser, Jacob 35
Kitely, Francis 35
Kittle, Thomas P. 35
Kline, John 121
  Mary M. 121
Knight, Jacob 35, 121, 158
Knott, James 35
  Nathaniel 36
Knox, John 35, 36
Koine, Dominick 122
  Mary 122

Kumy, John 19

L

Lamar, William 4
Lamb, Margaret 122
Lambert,
    Christopher 37, 122
Lanahan, Darby 36
Landers, Roger 36
Langford, Elijah 122, 158
Langrell, Timothy 37
Lanham, Kinsey 36
Lansdale, Cornelia 122
    Thomas 4, 122
Lantz, Jacob 121
Lapine, Paul 37
Larrimore, Thomas 37
Lashley, George 122
    Nancy 122
Laton, John 38
Laughlin, John M. 39
Laurence, Peter 38
Laurentz, Ann 122
    Vandel 122
Lavaschie, Ann 152
    Jno. 152
Lavender, John 38
Law, William 122, 158
Lawler, Michael 37
Laws, George 36
    Henry 36
    William 36
Layman, William 122, 145, 160
Leago, Charles 36
Leake, --- 122
    Henry 122
Leakins, William 37
Leary, Dennis 37
Leather, John 122, 158
Leddington, Peter 38
Lee, Dudley 37, 122, 123
    Jeremiah 38
    John 37
    Margaret 123
    Mary 123
    Parker 123
    William 36, 37
Leeke, --- 122
Legg, Edward 37
    Robert 37
LeGrande, Claudius 102
Leister, Joshua 37
Lemmon, Barney 38
LeNashu, John 4
Leonard, James 123, 160
Lesley, John 37
Lettman, William 36
Levi, Alexander 37
Lewin, John 37
Lewis, Jonathan 36
    Joseph 37
    Mary 123
    Richard 37
    Thomas 36
    William 123, 160
Lilly, William 36
Lindsay, John 38
    Theophilus 37
Lingan, James M. 4
    Jannet 123
    Thomas 123
Lingard, Nehemiah 37
Linkon, John 37
Linton, George 37
Lion, Jacob 38
Little, William 37
Livingston, Robert 37
Lloyd, Mary 123
    Michael 36
    Thomas 123, 160
Loar, George 88
Locker, Jesse 37
Loffman, Benjamin 36
Lomax, John 123, 160

Lomax, Theophilus 37
Lonass, John 36
Loney, Margaret 98
Long, Francis 37
  John 123
  Joseph 37
  Margaret 98
  Thomas 37
  William 123
Longest, Daniel 38
Lorantz, Elizabeth 124
  Ferdinand 124
Lord, Amelia 124
  Andrew 124, 158
  Henry 124, 160
  Levi 36
Love, David 37
  John 37
Loveday, John 36
  Thomas 37
Lovely, Joshua 37
  Thomas 37
Lovering, Peter 135
Lowe, Jacob 36
  John Tolson 4
Lower, Nathan A. 59
Lowry, James 38
  John 36
Lucas, Basil 124, 158
  John 36, 124, 160

Lucas, Rachel 124
  William 36
Luckett, David 4
  Thomas H. 4
Luff, John 38
  Thomas 38
Lyles, Zachariah 36
Lynch, Hugh 124, 158
  John 4, 37
  Thomas 124
  William 37
Lynn, David 4, 59, 69, 74, 87, 125
  Eleanor 124, 160
  Elizabeth 124
  George 61
  Jane 125
  John 4, 124, 160
  Mary 125
  Valentine 125
  William 68

M

M'Cann, Michael 160
M'Connell, Samuel 160
M'Gee, Charles 125, 160
  William 160
M'Kinsey, Moses 160
M'Pherson, Mark 160

M'Quinny, Thomas 160
Magee, Sarah 126
  William 126
Maglin, John 41
Magraw, James 38
  Stephen 39
Magruder, Nathaniel B. 126, 160
Maguire, Michael 39
  Peter 40
Mahoney, Clement 126, 160
  Edward 41, 160
  Thomas 39
Mahonney, Edward 126
Mahorn, Patrick 40
Majors, John 38
Malloy, Martin 43
Maloney, Luke 89
  Thomas 39
Managa, Joseph 40
Mangers, Nicholas 4
Manley, John 43
Manly, William 40
Mann, Daniel 41
  William 38, 40
Manning, Abraham 42
Mansfield, Henry 40
  William 41

Mantle, George 40
  John 38
Mantz, Catharine 126
  Peter 126
Marberry, Joseph 5
March, Charles 43
Markell, Jacob 62, 65, 67, 69, 73, 75, 77, 78, 80, 81, 82, 86
Markland, Alice 126
  Edward 126
Marlow, William 41
Marr, William 126
Marsh, Benjamin 41
  Charles 43
Marshal, William 38
Marshall, Benjamin 127
  John 127
Martin, Ann 149
  Ennals 127
  Henry 127
  Jacob 127
  John 39
  Margaret 127
  Sarah 127
  William 39
Martindale, John 39
Mason, Caleb 5
  Isachea 40

Mason, James 39
  Thomas 4
Massey, Hezikiah 38
Masterson, Phillip 42
Matthews, James 38
  John 38, 39
  Robert 38
  Thomas 40, 41
  William 42
Matthewson, Alex. 43
Mattingley, Henry 79
Mattingly, John 38
Maxwell, James 40, 127
  John 40
  Richard 42
May, Isaac 127
Mayer, C. F. 60
Mayhew, Eleanor L. 127
  Jonathan 38, 127, 160
Maylan, --- (Gen.) 117
Maynor, Peter 42
McAtee, Joseph 39
McAway, Christopher 40
McBride, John 42
McCaliff, John 41
McCann, Francis 41

McCann, John 40
  Michael 40, 125
Mccannally, John 40
McCarty, Edward 84
  Isaac 79, 84
  James 43
McCay, John 38
McCernan, Thomas 38
McClain, Arthur 38
  Enoch 40
  John 41
McColgan, John 43
McConnell, Samuel 38, 125
McConnikin, John 42
McCormick, Dennis 42
McCoy, Hugh 43
  John 5, 40, 113, 160
McCracken, James 125
  Mary 125
McCrakin, Jamer 43
McCulloh, James W. 70, 86
McDonald, George 43
  James 40
  John 39, 41
  Marmaduke 43

McDougle, John 42
McDowell, Hugh 42
McFadden, John H. 62
McFaden, James 5
  John H. 65
  John W. 71
McFadon, John H. 59, 69, 71, 73
  John W. 73
McGall, John 41
McGauran, Francis 41
McGee, Charles 39
  William 39, 125
McGin, James 77
McGirr, J. 77
  James 67
McGowen, John 42
McGower, Michael 39
McGran, John 42
McGraw, Christopher 39
McGuinis, John 40
McHaffee, Benjamin 39
McIntire, James 43
McIntosh, John 42
McKinley, William 42
McKinsey, Jesse 41
  Joshua 41
  Moses 41, 125
  Patrick 42
  Roderick 41

McKinsey, Sarah 125
  Thomas 42
McKnight, John 41
McLamar, Timothy 39
McLaughlin, Cornelius 39
  William 39
McLean, Arthur 125
McMahon, Barbara 99
  Timothy 42
McManiard, Nicholas 43
McManus, Barney 42
McMillan, Hugh 40
McNable, Charles 40
McNamara, Darby 39
  Joseph 38
McNaughton, Peter 39
McNeal, William 40
McNeill, John 41
McNemara, Darby 125, 126
McPherson, Mark 5, 126
  Samuel 4, 67
  Walter 126
  William 42

McQuinny, Thomas 126
Mead, James 40
Meadows, David 41
Meddagh, Frederick 127
Medlar, Bostian 128, 160
Medler, Boston 40
Melville, Aleard 41
Melvin, Peter 41
Merriam, Luke 41
Merrick, William 128, 160
Merryman, Elizabeth 128
  Luke 128
Michell, Aaron 41
Mick, John 40
Middleton, Gilbert 128
  Sarah 128, 160
Mie, Thomas 42
Milburn, Nicholas 40, 160
Miles, Frederick 38
  Jane 128
  John 38
  Joshua 128
  Walter 38
Miller, Benedict 85
  George 43, 128
  John 42, 75
  John C. 41
  Michael 39

Mills, Cornelius H.
  113, 160
  Elizabeth 111
  James 111
  John 40, 41
  Thomas 111
  Zachariah 42,
    128, 160
Milstead, John 42
Minikee, Gifford 38
Miniken,
  Humphrey 39
Minitree, Paul 128,
  160
Mitchel, Richard 39
Mitchell, Charles
    128
  John 4
  John H. 104
  Robert 41
  Walter H. S. 106
  William 40
Moade, William 40
Mollohon, Patrick
  42
Mondle, George
  128
Montle, George 128
Moore, Andrew 39
  James 42, 105
  John 38, 40, 41,
    128
  Mary 129
  Matthew 40
  Nicholas R. 129

Moore, Nicholas
    Ruxton 128
  Rueben 129, 160
  Samuel T. 129
  Sarah 128, 129
  William 39, 40,
    129
  Zedikaih 5
Moran, Benjamin
  39
Morgan, David 5
  Thomas 42
Morris, John 4, 38,
  41, 129
  Jonathan 129
  Neal 40
Morrison, John 39
Morton, Archibald
  42
  L. M. 61
  Laurence M. 61
  Lawrence M. 76
  M. 61
  William 61, 72,
    83
Moser, Cruise 42
Moses, Jacob 39,
  42
Moudle, George
  160
Moutle, George 160
Mudd, Ann 129
  Barbara 129
  Bennet 39, 160
  Bennett 129
  Jeremiah 38

Mudd, Richard 38
Muir, Thomas 129
Muiritt, Charles 42
Murdoch, William
  7
Murdock, Benjamin
    129, 160
  Patrick 130
  William 130
Murley, Dennis 42
Murphey, Joseph
  40
Murphy, Charles
    39
  Daniel 41
  James 42
  Thomas 40
Murray, John 41,
    42
  Valentine 38
Muse, Walker 5
Mushler, Adam 41
Myers, Christian 39
  Jacob 42
  Lawrence 5
  Robert 42
Myres, Christian 5

N

Nabb, Charles 43
  Joseph 43
Nagle, Richard 130
Nailor, William 43
Narvel, James 43
Nave, John 44

191

Naylor, Henry 73, 77, 82
Neagell, Morris 43
Neal, Daniel 44
Neale, Eleanor 130
 Henry 130
 James 44, 130
 Joseph 44
 Wilmore 69
Neary, John 43
Needham, William A. 130
Needhand, William A. 43
Neighbors, John 43
Neill, Thomas 43
Nelme, Samuel J. 44
Nelson, Eliza 130
 James 132
 John 5, 43
 Richard 43
 Roger 5, 130
Nevit, John 44
Newman, John 130, 160
Newton, John 43, 130, 160
 William 43
Niblet, John 130
 William 43, 160
Nicholls, Asael 43
 Isaac 43
Nicholson, George 44
 Henry 43

Nicholson, John 44
 Nicholas 43
 Stephen 43
Noble, Martin 44
Nolan, Patrick 43
Noland, Michael 43
Norman, Basil 43
Norris, Jacob 5
Norwood, Edward 119
 Samuel 77
Nott, Nathaniel 44
Nourse, Charles 59
Nowell, James 131, 160

O

O'Boyle, John B. 113
O'Bryan, Dennis 131
O'Conner, Michael 162
O'Connor, Michael 131
O'Farrel, Michael 44
O'Hara, John 131
 Susan 131
O'Quinn, Daniel 44
O'Quynn, Richard 44
Oakley, Elijah 44
Obrian, John 44
 Michael 44
 Philip 44

Oldham, Edward 5
Oliver, R. 69
 Robert 66, 68
Onants, James 44
Onion, John 44
 Juliet 131
Oram, Samuel 44
Orem, Spedden 131
Orme, Charles 44
 Moses 131
Orndorff, Christian 131, 162
Osborn, John 44
Osten, Henry 44
Ott, Adam 131, 162
 Juliana 131
Outerbridge, Leonard 44
Outhouse, Peter 44
Overereck, Joseph 44
Owens, Gassaway 108
 Jacob 44
 James 44
 John 44
 Joseph 44
 Samuel 44
 Stephen 44

Pack, James 46
Pagram, William 46
Paine, John 46

Painter, Mary 131
  Melchoir 131
Paivel, James 46
Parker, James 44
Parkinson, John 46
Parran, Jane 131
  Thomas 131
Parrish, Edward 132
Parrot, Christopher 132
Parsons, John 46
Pasterfield, Philip 91
Patten, Coleman 132
Patterson, Thomas 46
Pattrick, George 45
Paul, Catharine 132
  Thomas 132
  William 46
Peacock, Neal 45, 132
  Neale 162
  Thomas 45
Peak, Nathan 44
Peany, John 45
Pearce, Aquilla 45
  George 132
Pearcy, James 78
Pearsonm, John 46
Pease, John 45
Pecker, William 45

Pegegram, William 132
Pen, John 162
Pendergast, William 5, 131
Penefield, Hester 132
  Thomas 132
Penn, John 132
Pennington, Robert 46
Pennyfield, Thomas 45
Pepper, Elijah 45
Perry, George C. 69
  Lucy 59, 61, 66, 77, 81
  Simon 45
  Thomas 46, 59
Peters, Gabriel 45
  Joseph 46
  William 45
Pettit, Thomas 46
Phelps, Benjamin 46
Pherson, Joseph 46
  William 45
Philips, Stephen 132, 162
Phillips, George 45
  Henry 44
  James 45
  Jonas 46
  Lambert 45
Phipps, Thomas 45

Pickering, John 45
Pierce, George 45
  Joshua 46
Pilkerton, Michael 46
Pindell, Gassaway 132
  Nicholas 132
  Richard 5, 132, 162
Pinder, Thomas 45
Pixel, Jacob 70
Plaine, Jacob 46
Plane, Catherine 133
  Jacob 133
Pleasants, Samuel 45
Plumley, George 45
Plummer, Cupid 44
  Obadiah 45
Poe, Elizabeth 133, 162
Pogue, Joseph 46
Poland, William 45
Pollard, Thomas 60
Pollhouse, Thomas 45
Polston, Emanuel 46
Poole, James 45
Popha, Francis 46
Popham, Benjamin 133
Porter, Nathan 133
  Thomas 46

Porter, William 46
Potter, Thomas 46
Powers, Jesse 45, 133, 162
  Milly 133
Prall, Edward 5
Prather, William 46
Preston, Andrew 46
  Stephen 45
Price, Benjamin 5
  George 133
  Nathaniel 46
  Stephen 45
  Stephen R. 133
  Thomas 5, 46
Prior, William 45
Pritchard, James 46
Pritchet, Arthur 46
Proctor, Richard 45, 133, 162
Prout, John 46
Pruitt, Walter 133
Purchase, William 45
Purdy, Edward 46
  Henry 45
  John 45
  Joseph 45
Pursell, William 45

Q

Quay, James 47, 105
Queen, Marsham 133
Quick, John 46
Quinn, John 46, 47
  Patrick 47
Quinny, Thomas M. 133
Quinton, William 46

R

Radley, John 47
Raines, Adam 47
Raison, William 5
Ramsay, Daniel 106
Ramsey, Nathaniel 5
Rasin, William B. 133
Rawlings, Ann 133
  Anne 162
  Bennet 47
  Isaac 5
  Samuel 133
  Solomon 134
Ray, Joseph 134, 162
Raybolt, Jacob 5
Reading, Henry 162
Redman, Thomas 47
Reed, Philip 5
Reid, John 134
Reiley, William 162
Reily, Barbara 134

Reily, William 134
Revely, Francis 5
Reynolds, Benedict 47
  Charles 47
  James 134
  Ruth 134
  Tobias 134, 162
Rhytmire, Michael 47
Richards, Mary 134
  Paul 134
Richardson,
  Charles 134, 162
  Daniel 134, 162
  David 124
  Edward 47
  Elizabeth 124
  Nancy 134, 162
  Robert 47
  William 47
Richmond,
  Christopher 5
Ricketts, Nicholas 5
Riddle, Charles 47
Ridgely, Eli 74, 80
  John H. 84
  William 130
Riely, Edward 47
  William 5
Rigby, William 135, 162
Riggs, Andrew 47

Risdon, Cassandra 135
  Zadock 135
Rise, Robert 47
Riston, Benjamin 135
  Zadock 135
Roading, Henry 134
Robbins, John 135, 162
Roberts, Horatio 47
  Jane 135
  Mary 135
  William 47, 135, 162
  Zachariah 135
Robertson, Eleanor 135
  John 47
Robinson, Standly 135
Robosson, Charles 135
  Rebecca 135
Roby, John 135, 162
Rock, John 47
  William 47
Rodes, Jeremiah 47
Rogers, William 47
Rolle, Robert 136
Ross, Cristian 47
Rouark, James 136
  Julia 136
Rouse, Thomas 5
Rowie, Thomas 162
Rowles, William 47
Rowse, Thomas 136
Roxburgh, Alexander 5
Ruark, Barbara 136
  James 136
Rudloph, John 5
Rudolph, Michael 5
Rutherford, Alexander 47
Rutledge, John 5
  Joshua 96, 136
Ryly, James 47

S

Salmon, John 49
Salsbury, Thomas 51
Sandall, John 51
Sanders, George 49
  John 52
  Thomas 47
Sankey, John 52
Sansbury, John 136
  Sarah 136
Sanson, Luke 50
Sappington, Cassandra 136
  James 51
  Richard 136
  Thomas 48
Savage, Robinson 94
Savoy, Philip 50
Schley, F. A. 69
Schoudrick, Charles 48
Schrach, Andrew 136
Scone, George 51
Scott, Charles 49
  David 81
  Elizabeth 136, 137
  James 51
  John 49
  Levi 50
  Patrick 52
  Rueben 51
  Samuel 48, 136, 137, 162
  William 137
Scoudrick, Thomas 51
Scrabbles, Jeremiah 52
Scriviner, Robert 48
Scrivner, Sarah 137
Seaburn, John 137, 162
Sears, John 6, 137
  Mary 137
  Noah 48
Seaton, W. W. 86
Second, George 137, 162

Sellman, Jonathan 6
Semmes, Anne 93
  James 137, 162
Sergeant, Thomas 52
Sewall, Charles 137, 164
  James 49, 164
Sewell, Clement 137
  James 137
  Rebecca 137
  William 137, 164
Seymore, Christopher 50
Shane, Henry 137
  Henry W. 137
Shanks, John 50
Sharp, William 48
Sharpless, Robert 49
Shaur, James 49
Shaw, Basil 51
  John 52
  Joseph F. 115
  William 139
Shean, Henry 137
Shee, Murphy 48
Sheets, Hannah 138
Sheffer, John 50
Shepherd, James 50
Sherburn, Charles 138

Sherburn, Mary 138
Sheredine, John 95
Sheridan, Barthelolomew 52
  James 52
  Thomas 51
Sherley, Bennet 50
  William 48
Shipley, Robert 48
Shircliff, Leonard 138
  Melinda 138
  William 138
Shirley, Bennett 138
  Susanna 138
Shockee, Abraham 48
Shoebrick, Phillip 52
Shoebrook, Edward 138
Shoemaker, Jacob 6
  Peter 52
  Samuel F. 51
Sholts, John 164
Short, Jonathan 48
Shorter, Roger 49
Shotts, John 138
Shouell, John 49
Shrink, Andrew 51
Shryack, John 138

Shryer, Mary C. 121
Shugart, Martin 6
Sickle, Charles 50
Sidmer, Joseph 50
Sidney, Joseph 50
Sillman, John 51
Silver, George 48
Silwood, William 50
Simmonds, James 51
Simmons, Aaron 138, 164
  Noble 52
  Sarah 138
  William 48
Simms, James 52
Simons, Jesse 47
Simpkins, Christopher 50
  John 67
Simpson, Charles 52
  Laurence 50
  Lawrence 138, 164
  Mary 139
  Rezin 138, 139, 162
  Thomas 139
Sinclair, Alexander 60
  Robert 89
  William 49

Sizeland, William 51
Sizler, Philip 139
Skerrilt, Clement 6
Skiventon, Roger 96
Slack, Henry 51
  John 51
Slade, Thomas 49
Slicer, Andrew 149
  George 64
Sloop, John 52
  Joseph 49
Sly, William 48
Smallwood, John 50
  Walter B. 51
  William 5
Smith, Alex H. 5
  Alex. 6
  Alexander 48, 61
  Alexander Lawson 119, 139
  Andrew 48
  Anthony 47
  Aquilla 48, 139
  Benjamin 48, 139
  Charles 139
  Christian 51, 162
  Christopher 51
  Clement 78, 84
  Conrad 49
  Daniel 49, 50
  David 47
  Edward M. 6
Smith, Eichael 51
  Elias 50
  Elijah 49, 139, 164
  Elizabeth 116
  Ephraim 139
  George 61
  James 6, 49, 51, 68, 87
  John 6, 48, 49, 50, 51, 52, 139, 140, 164
  John A. 82, 84
  Joseph 6, 48, 140
  Josiah 48
  Leonard 48, 83
  Levy 49
  Mary 139
  Michael 50
  Nathaniel 52, 140
  Peter 49
  Priscilla 139
  Richard 48
  Robert 51
  Rueben 48
  Sarah 140
  Thomas 48, 49, 50, 51, 140
  Valentine 51
  William 47, 49, 52
Smithard, John 48
Smoot, William 6
Smyth, Anna M. 140
  Thomas 140
Snelling, John 47
Snow, Charles 52
Snowden, Cato 51
Somervell, James 140
Somerville, James 6
Sours, Michael 48
Southall, Joseph 51
Spalding, Aaron 49, 162
  Henry 162
Spaulding, Aaron 140
  Daniel 141
  Henry 141
  Samuel 141
Speak, Nathan 48
Spedden, Ann 141
  Edward 141, 164
Spencer, Humphrey 49
  Joseph H. 51
  Tamerlane 52
Spiker, Solomon 82
Spinks, Joseph 52
  Rawling 51
Spire, John 50
Spires, Richard 50, 141
Sprigg, M. C. 142
Spriggs, John 52
Sproul, Mary 122
Spurrier, Edward 6
Spyers, William 52

Stackhouse, John 48
Stalker, William 51
Stallins, Abraham 50
Standley, Jacob 51
  John 51
  Thomas 51
  William 51
Standly, Michael 49
Stanford, Constance D. 116
  Nancy 116
Stanley, Salday 50
Stanton, John 51, 141
  William 84
Staples, John 141, 164
  Margaret 141
Starkey, John 50
Steem, George 49
Stephens, Levi 141, 142, 162
  Oliver 51
  Peter 50
  Polly 141
Stephenson, Alexander 49
  William B. 104
Sterling, William 50
Steuart, Elizabeth 141

Stevens, Benjamin 141, 162
  David 141
  Levi 141
  William W. 141
Steward, Benjamin 50
  William 50
Stewart, Andrew 48
  D. 86
  David 70
  James 48
  John 6
Stoddert, Benjamin 60
  William T. 6
Stoffe, John 50
Stoffee, Frederick 48
Stoffle, John 50
Stokes, Thomas 48
Stone, John 142
  John H. 5
Stonestreet, William 49
Storer, Dorothy 114, 142
Strahan, John 52
Strap, Jacob 142
Street, Samuel 50
Streets, Robert 50
Strider, Philip 142
Stuart, Elizabeth 141

Studer, Philip 142, 162
Stumm, George 49
Sturton, Robert 52
Suite, Jesse 49
Sullivan, Darby 52
  James 50
  Jeremiah 48
  Perry 49
  Solomon 50
  William 49
Summers, John 49
  Solomon 49, 142, 162
  Thomas 50
Summerville, George 52
Sute, Edward 48
Sutton, Abraham 52
  Charles 51
Swan, James 65, 72, 79, 81
  John 6, 63, 70, 75, 78, 83, 84
  Leonard 47, 142
  Robert 139
Swann, James 68
  Leonard 164
Swearingen, Elie 79
Sweeny, James 52
  Richard 52
Sykes, William 49
Sylvester, Job 50
  Thomas 52

T

Tanehill, Josiah 6
Tannehill,
   Adomson 6
   Agnes M. 142
Tanner, Edward 54
   Thomas 53
Tasco, Richard 53
Tasker, Richard 142
   Richard R. 164
Taylor, Francis 54
   George 53
   John 53, 143
   Mary 164
   Richard 52, 143, 164
   Robert 53
   Samuel 53
   Sega 143
   Sydney 143
   William 53
Templeman,
   George 59, 60, 61, 70, 72, 73, 74, 79, 83, 86
   John 89
   Richard W. 76
Ternan, Dennis 54
Terry, James 53
Thacknill, Rezin 54
Thayer, Stephen 65
Thistle, Archibald 64
Thomas, Evan 54

Thomas, Francis 77
   Giles 53
   James 53
   John 54
   John German 54
   John Jarman 143
   Joseph 143, 164
   Levin 53
   Richard 103
   Thomas 54
Thompsen,
   Lambert 53
Thompson, Barnard 143
   Charles 143, 164
   Clement 133
   Francis 53
   Giles 53
   Israel 87
   Jesse 54, 143, 164
   John 143
   Joseph 54
   Lewis 65
   Mary 143, 164
   Thomas 53, 143
Tigner, James 54
Tillard, --- (Col.) 143
   Edward 6, 113
   Otho Thomas 143
   Sarah 143, 164
   Taylor 164
Tillotson, Thomas 143, 144
Timms, Edward 52

Tindall, Samuel 54
Tippet, Natley 53
   Peter 53
Tite, James 53
Toland, William 53
Tomlin, John 53
Tompson,
   Bartholomew 53
Tomson, Cornelius 53
   John 54
Toomey, John 144
Toonry, John 164
Topham, Benjamin 97
Topping, Peter 53
Touchstone,
   Christopher 53
Towlin, John 54
Townley, Henry 53
Townsend, Aaron 54
   Allen 144, 164
   Granville S. 122
   Thomas 144
   William 52
Townshend,
   Catharine 67
Towsend, Allen 53
Towson, William 7
Tramwell, Dennis 52
Trego, James 54
Trigg, Samuel 53
Truck, John 144

Trueman,
   Alexander 6
   John 6, 144
Trusty, John 53
Trux, Elizabeth 144
   John 144
Tucker, Anthony 53
   Henry 54
   John 52
Tuff, John 54
Tully, John D. 54
Tumbleson, Evin 53
Turner, John 53, 54
   Solomon 53
   Thomas 144, 164
Tutten, William 54
Tutwiller, Jonathan 131, 144, 164
Twench, George 54
Tyack, Thomas 54
Tycowit, Francis 54
Tydings, Kealy 144

U

Uncles, Benjamin 144, 166
   Rebecca 144
Usselton, William 93

V

Valdenar, Frances 145
Van Buskirk, Samuel 82
Vane, James 145
   John 144
   Lucretia 144, 145
Vanzant, John 54
Varlow, John 54
   Stephen 54, 145, 164
Vaughan, Cornelius 54
   John 55
   William 54
Vaughn, William 145, 164
Veazy, James 55
Vermillion, Samuel 54
Vernon, George 55
Vickers, Edward 54
Vincent, John 54

W

Wade, Edward 56
   John 56
   William 58
Walker, John 57, 145, 166
   Mary 145
   Robert 56
Wall, Edward 58
   Keturah 145
   Kitturah 145
   William 145, 166
Walley, Mary 145
   Thomas 145
   Zedikiah 145
Walls, Martha 146
Walter, Edward 57
Waltman, Mary 146
   Michael 57, 146
Waltz, Henry 71
Ward, Benjamin 55
   George 55
   John 58
   Peter 58
Ware, Francis 6, 146
Warfield, Walter 6
Waring, Basil 7
Warren, James 64
Warring, Ann 146
   Basil 146
Warrior, Daniel 56
Warters, Abraham 58
Washington, George 117
Wate, Thomas 56
   William 6
Waters, Elizabeth J. 146
   J. G. W. 60
   John 58
   Jonathan 146, 166
   Margaret 146

Waters, Richard 6, 146, 164
Wilson 146
York 55
Watkins, Gassaway 6, 113, 146, 164
Leonard 146, 164
Mary 146
William 57
Wats, James 146
Watson, George 56
Sarah Ann 146
Thomas 56
Walter 55
William H. 146
Watts, Solomon 58
Weaver, Anthony 57
Webb, Banks 57
Webster, Thomas 58
Wedge, Samuel 57
William 55
Weeden, Jonathan 55
Weily, Richard 57
Welch, David 58
Garret 58
James 57, 58
John 56, 57
Nicholas 56
Wells, Humphrey 57
John 57
Martha 147

Wells, William 136
Welsh, Phillip 55
Weltner, Ludowick 7
West, Alexander 55
Benjamin 147
James 57
John 57
John T. 56
William 55
Whaland, William 56
Whaley, Zadock 57
Whaling, James 57
Wheatley, Rhoda 147
Sylvester 55
William 55, 147
Wheeler, Charles 57
John 58
Mary 147
Nathaniel 147
Richard 55
Thomas 58
Wheland, Mary 100
Whetstone, Daniel 86
Jacob 86
Samuel 86
Whilhelm, Jacob 67
Whitaker, William 137
Whitcomb, James 55
Motley 55

White, David 57
Edward 58
George 166
Henry 85
James 57, 147
Jonathan 56
Joseph 55
Priscilla 147
Richard 122
Samuel B. 55, 147
Sarah 147
Thomas 147
William 79
Whittaker, William 57
Whitton, William 57
Wiery, Elizabeth 147
Michael 56, 147
Wiland, William 61
Wiley, Holmes 83
John 60
Wilkenson, John 56
Wilkerson, John 55
Young 147
Wilkeson, William 55
Wilkinson, James 147, 164
Young 7, 164
Willett, Charles 56
Williams, Benjamin 56, 57

Williams, Charles 55, 147, 164
    Daniel 55
    David 55
    Elisha 147
    Gabriel 55
    George 57
    Harriet 147
    James 57, 58
    Jarvis 57
    Jeremiah 56
    John 55, 56, 148, 166
    Joseph 148
    Lilburn 6
    Nancy 114
    Nathan 7
    Osborn 148
    Otho Holland 6
    Thomas 57
    Zachariah 58
Willin, Charles 135
    Levin 148
Willing, John 55, 56
Willins, Evans 148
Willis, Andrew 148, 166
    Daniel 56
    Esther 147
    John 56
    Lethe 148
Willmot, Robert 148
Willson, Benjamin 58
Willson, David 56
    George 55
    James 56, 57
    John 57
    Samuel 57
    William 55, 57, 58
Wilmot, Robert 6, 96
    William 6
Wilmott, Frederick 56
Wilson, Barney 56
    David 148, 166
    Jonathan 72
    Michael 65, 88
    Rachel 148
    Thomas 81
    Thos. 79, 85
Wimber, Thomas 56, 148
Winbrough, Leah 149
    Thomas P. 149
Winchester, George 7
    James 6
Windell, Jonathan 55
Winder, Levin 6
Windom, Thomas 56
Wingate, Andrew 55
Winham, George 55
Wiser, Michael 55
Withorm, William 57
Wolcott, William 149
Wood, Gerard 6
    James 56, 57
    John 30
    Robertson 56
    Thomas 56
Woodland, Rhody 57
Woods, David 58
Wooford, Thomas 6
Woolford, Michael 56
    Priscilla 113
    Thomas 55
    William 6
Workman, Isaac 87
Wright, Absolum 56
    Ann 149
    Edward 55, 149
    Jesse 56, 149, 164
    John 57
    Nathan 7
    Samuel 55
    Samuel T. 149
Wyatt, Thomas 56
Wycall, Adam 149
Wykall, Adam 149
Wyndham, Sarah 149, 166
Wysham, John 58

Y

Yates, Richard 58
　Thomas 149
Yeast, Jacob 58
Yeates, Thomas 58
York, William 58
Yost, Jacob 58
Young, Benjamin
　　149, 166
　David 58
　Godfrey 58
　Henry 58
　Jacob 58
　John 58
　Samuel 58

Other Heritage Books by Mary K. Meyer:

A Directory of Cayuga County Residents Who Supported Publication of the History of Cayuga County, New York

Abstracts from Madison County, New York Newspapers in the Cazenovia Public Library

Baltimore City Birth Records, 1865–1894

Cemetery Inscriptions of Madison County, New York, Volume 1
Mary K. Meyer and Joyce C. Scott

Divorces and Names Changed in Maryland by Act of the Legislature, 1634-1867

Free Blacks in Harford, Somerset and Talbot Counties, Maryland 1832

Meyer's Directory of Genealogical Societies in the U.S.A. and Canada: 1998–2000, 12th Edition
Family of Mary K. Meyer

Westward of Fort Cumberland: Military Lots Set Off for Maryland's Revolutionary Soldiers

Who's Who in Genealogy and Heraldry 1990
Mary K. Meyer and P. William Filby

www.ingramcontent.com/pod-product-compliance
Lightning Source LLC
Chambersburg PA
CBHW051922160426
43198CB00012B/2005